In Praise of BOF

"What a gift, this book. Borealis Mundi i
into connection with more of ourselves.
intimate relationship with all we encoun
of our soul home."

> – Chelan Harkin, author of Susceptible to Light and Let Us Dance,
> The Stumble and Whirl with The Beloved

"With great love, sumptuous prose, lyric poetry, and well-honed storytelling, Tracy guides us through the chaotic storms and emotional shoals that forged her journey and her life. Borealis Mundi is a visceral, spiritual odyssey across literal and psychic waters. Those acquainted with grief and loss will hear echoes of their own lives in her stories. And they may find wisdom there as well. I know I did."

> – Kevin McMullin, author of Into the Black Sea -
> Stories of Darkness & Light www.kevinmcmullin.com

"It takes courage for a writer to allow the message of a book to create the form of the book. It also takes courage to walk through life awake to its darkness and its light simultaneously. Tracy Chipman's wonderful book exemplifies this sort of courage. A very important voice of the feminine lies between these pages."

> – Nancy Swisher, MA, MFA, author of The Life That Woke Me Up Was My Own,
> Founder of Find Your Voice Women's Club at nancyswisher.com

"Luminescent, gritty, vulnerable, elegant, raw. This memoir is full of the soul's might."

> – Cybele, spiritual counselor and author of Love Song

"*Borealis Mundi is a treasure of a book. It carries readers beyond heart-breaking loss and through the labyrinth of profound transformation. With the warmth, delight, and honesty of a close friend, Tracy Chipman tells her story of soul discovery with the wisdom, courage, and love that will support your own life journey.*"

– Anthony Lawlor, author of *A Home for The Soul*
and *The Temple in The House*

"*This memoir is luminous. Wrought through the devastation of loss, Borealis Mundi is an offering of profound vulnerability and grace of connection—with place, with other humans and more-than-humans, and within ourselves, all kin, all a part of "the elements surrounding, engulfing, becoming," like "the great inland sea," the author's navigator North Star, the beloved Lake Superior, Gichi-gami.*"

– Carter McKenzie is the author of a chapbook of poetry and two full-length collections of poetry, the most recent of which is *Stem of Us* (Flowstone Press, 2018). She is an active member of SURJ (Showing Up for Racial Justice).

"*Bravery, power, insight, and beauty: in a memoir which includes poetry, immersive nature writing, and an astonishing story of unthinkable tragedy, grief, and recovery. Tracy's courage and skill bring a story of healing and connection.*"

– Tom Morton, writer and broadcaster, author of *Holy Waters*

"*Tracy Chipman has a rare combination of gifts—storyteller, mystic's sensibility, and a poet's exuberant delight in language. Add a heart broken open by grief, and you have the recipe for a transcendental piece of work. When Tracy writes about death, life, and immersion in the wild, she can be breathtaking. In Borealis Mundi, she takes us into philosophical territory, without losing her conversational tone. Her voice, will stay with me a long time.*"

– Jackie Singer, storyteller and author of *Birthrites, Rituals and Ceremonies for the Child-Bearing Years*

BOREALIS MUNDI

RESTING IN PLACE, LOSS, AND GRACE

A MEMOIR

Tracy Chipman

Little Big Bay LLC

5% of proceeds will go to organizational efforts: supporting women's reproductive
rights, environmental, and anti-racist endeavors.

For additional information: tlchipman@gmail.com

Author: Tracy Chipman tracychipman.net

Cover image: Elena Ray
Section images: Tracy Chipman
Book designer: Roslyn Nelson

Publisher: LittleBigBayShop.com

Fonts: Mrs.Eaves, designed by Zuzana Licko
Trajan, designed by Carol Twombly
Avenir, designed by Adrian Frutiger

ISBN: 979-8-218-16556-7

"NOT KNOWING
WHEN THE DAWN
WILL COME,
I OPEN
EVERY DOOR."

– Emily Dickinson

Dedicated to those who listen, love, and tell from the fringes,
the Truth-sayers, Shift-shapers, and the Broken Brights,
and to my Ancestors, those in whom I root.

Blood Ancestors

Lorna: Leona and Lorin, Magdalena and William, Laura, and Arthur
Wayne: Rose and Willis, Regina and William, Edith, and Chancy Bird ...

Land Ancestors

Those Indigenous human beings of the near and far past who have
inhabited landscapes that have known me: the Potawatomi,
Anishinaabe, Ho Chunk, Dine, Anasazi, and Oceti Sakowin Peoples.
The Chelamela, Siuslaw, and Kalapuya Peoples. The Celts, and the Pictish
Peoples. Honoring the memory, the lives, the trauma, and atrocities
committed by colonialists, by my European blood ancestors and the
patriarchal, religious, capitalistic conditionings they wittingly or
unwittingly upheld and those more-than-human beings; animal,
vegetable, mineral, rhizomal.

Soul Ancestors

Beings, human and more-than-human, who have touched, inspired, and
deeply informed my life's soul journey; those who have crossed over—some
I have known personally and many who lived in the deep past and/or whom
I've never met. A few of my soul ancestors include: Venus–a beloved black
cat, Enheduanna, Diana Spencer, Seumas MacLeod, Boadicea/Buddug,
Vivian Laport, Cathie Walker, Joan of Arc, Albert Einstein, Maharishi
Mahesh Yogi, Bruce Beal, Allan Watts, Donnie MacRury, Zora Neale Hurston,
Mary Oliver, Ursula Le Guin, Don Ekstrom, and the long list of women/men
accused and killed for "being witches."

～

In whom do you root?

Dear Reader

T hank you for holding this book in your hands, settling yourself somewhere and opening here. May that opening be a resting into animate places, lived losses and into the numinous grace we are part of.

Borealis mundi is Latin for northern worlds. Latin was traditionally not spoken by people in community; it was not a mother tongue. In choosing a Latin title, it is my small attempt at retrieving Latin from its often dark history of privileged use and weaving it into common vernacular. Borealis mundi reflects my continued inquiry and a deeper habitation of northern places: geographical, ancestral, and personal.

Throughout the book I use multiple pronouns; she, he, they, ki, and kin interchangeably, reflecting my relationship with the panoply of life.

On these pages are my humble alchemical attempts at this time and place, exploring what humans have always done: listened and listened, and then sung, told, left their mark on a cave wall, a canvas or a page—making the dark into art.

I am an oral storyteller; telling stories—ancient and new—is part of my singular way of being in the world. And in this time of great transformation I offer these written narratives, essays, and poems of transformation to you, and us. The offerings in this book, often non-linear, metaphysical, and born of liminal experiences, reflect an ontological shift in my way of being in and with the animate world. Perhaps these expressions will be a compass in your transformation, in the great transformation we are all part of. Some pieces may confound or trouble you, some validate and delight. Some may find you holding the terrible and the beautiful in both hands, celebrating your aliveness.

May what rests within these pages, within us and between us, be acknowledged as the compost essential to sow deeper intimacies with our lives and with the living world. May we open to hear what we are ready to hear, to feel what we are ready to feel, and know what we are ready to know. With deep, deep gratitude to all my relations.

Tracy
Washburn Wisconsin, September 2022

Weaver at the End of the World

*Life is no definite thing with a beginning and an end, a growth
and a climax, but a basket of fragments, passages that lead to nothing,
curious incidents which look of importance at first but which crumble
and break into pieces, dropping into ruins.*

– Margaret Oliphant

T he bleak winter world was waking, the sweet sap was rising
throughout the boreal forests of the north woods and I too
was emerging from a seven-year stretch of winter, a dark night of
the soul. Over those seven years of shadow and shine, from 2009
to 2016, I would revel in and release deep ties to ancestral lands in
rural Northcentral Wisconsin, coming to know a new peace and
strength within. I would bow to the majesty of the bright waters of
Lake Superior, the sanctuary shores of Lake Menomin, and I'd revisit
the gifts given to me in my youth by the people, language, and lands
of Scotland.

In the middle of that seven-year conversation, broken open by
loss after loss, I was on the fragile cusp of a new cycle and a new
chapter. I was just beginning to grow into a new skin. In that fertile
place, a story found me, told to me by a woman whom I greatly
admire. We shared a love of Scottish isles, deep myth, and Celtic
consciousness. This story's arrival was perfectly on time, as they
most often are. Over thousands of miles I listened to her tell a

story, ancient and new, virtual and live, from Scotland, every word soaking into the marrow my bones.

In Scottish Gaelic, the word *cailleach* means older woman. Cailleach can refer to the older woman living next door, the wise woman, spey-wife of many folk stories, and to the powerful mythic hag-crone, the Cailleach–the Celtic guardian of wisdom, of winter, of death. She is the creatrix and destructress. Some believe she is the very land herself, often found betwixt and between the edges and cul-de-sacs of time and place.

This story, one of many stories about the Cailleach, has been a lifeline through many years of alchemy. Variations of this story are rooted in my bones, have spun from my lips in my life's work as an oral storyteller and spilled into the imaginations of hundreds through the liminal magic of storytelling. Here is my iteration of this Celtic story.

At the edge and end of a great inland sea, there is a great gash, a mouth, a womb, a cave, in the billions of years-old stone. There, 10,000 spiders spin their fairy tale threads. Webs frame and cloak the cave's mouth until they are swept away by wild gusts of wind. The spiders begin afresh, spin and weave, spin and weave. Inside, the red granite cave is ceaselessly scoured by wind and wave, and the drip, drip of water, salty and sweet. This is a shadowed place blooming in moss and lichen, skittering with centipedes, a cave sun-bright with the light of stories, ancient and newly born. In this cave the old Cailleach—the Goddess Crone of Winter, of life and death, dwells.

The Cailleach is a weaver. She weaves the tapestry of the universe—the great, always flowing story, from threads of fine silk ribbons, ragged flax, filthy rags, and hand-spun wool. She weaves down and in, under and through. She weaves us, and everything in between. She weaves All.

In the cave which echoes the magnificent song of the sea, she sits. There on her loom of ancient oak, she weaves. Her breath the wind, her moon-silver hair a river ratted with gorse twigs and birch bark. Her lungs a forest, her breasts autumn meadows, and her face etched by 10,000 stories.

In the cave of moss and stone, spiders spin and bats dream, and there at the end of the world, the gnarled apple branches of her arms and hands weave—down and in, under and through. The Cailleach draws from the great tangled heap of wool, rag, silk, and bone. She has always been here in this place, weaving. This is her task in life. Her gift to all.

As she weaves, whole body poised, she listens. She listens with her eyes, and she listens with her heart. She listens with her yoni, and she listens with her breath. She hears us all and then she weaves. As she weaves, she sings, she howls, she curses, and with the starlight pouring in, she often weeps, as the stories are born in the warp and weft of the Great Cloth.

In the center of the cave there is a fire and there sits a great stone cauldron holding the essence and intelligence of every living entity—animal, mycelial, vegetable, mineral—which roils and froths in one hearty, holy elixir.

The Cailleach is also tasked to tend this brew ... and time and time again, she gets so engrossed in the weaving, she forgets. She forgets until the perfume of things scorched reaches her nose. At that, she jumps from the loom, hirpling toward the fire, her hoary bones clattering as she moves. At the edge of the fire, she lifts a spurtle as big as an oar and begins to stir the pot, praying that it does not spoil. She stirs, and stirs, salt-sweat streams from her brow.

"Please do not let this precious brew be burned." She murmurs, sings, and prays.

Now, as she toils and prays, there in a crack in the cave, two coal black eyes watch this holy commotion. It is Raven. Raven has been waiting and watching for a long, long time. She has been waiting for this very moment.

As the long shadows flicker over the walls of rock and moss, of memory and time, Raven launches herself from the crack in the wall, her black feathers a luminous shroud surging across the cave. She lands on the loom. She cocks her head, eyeing the Great Cloth of stories. She gets a good eyeful and Raven does what Raven does best—she begins to pick and pull, rip and tear, thread by thread, tugging and destroying the fine weaving. What has taken epochs to create is ruined in the blink of an eye. Raven eyes the chaos she has made. She chuckles and preens—her feathers revealing sparks of every color. Then as silently as she arrived, she lifts off the loom, wings wide as she glides, back to her crack in the wall. Back to her snug to wait and watch.

The Cailleach sees none of this, so absorbed she is in the stirring of the cauldron. Her toil has paid off, the brew has been saved. Pausing, her chin resting on the head of the spurtle, she catches her breath, stills her heart and then before going back to the loom, she gives thanks to the 10,000 allies all around.

At the loom, she is met with Raven's handiwork of destruction; all her work, all the stories, the Great Cloth utterly ravaged. All her effort and cunning and craft—all gone. With a howl, she drops to her knees and in that wild tangle of color and texture, she weeps. All the bones in Cailleach's body shake as she keens for what has been lost. Salt tears soak and sooth, flow and flood until she is empty, until nothing is left. In that thunderous silence, a newly minted peace blooms, like spores releasing in the dark cave.

After a timeless time, when her grief is clean, when even the busy spiders of the cave rest, the old crone rests until her eyes spy spider. Spider, now awake, drops from the ceiling of the cave into the whole mess before her. The holy Hag's gaze follows and lands on one woolen crimson thread knotted in the chaos. This thread, this ruby-red thread of finely spun wool is the most intoxicating color she has ever seen. She reaches her bony fingers into the tangle. She tugs and tenderly pulls this crimson thread from the nest of fiber. She smells the sweet comfort of the wool, brings the thread to her lips, and tastes the salt of her tears. Then, with her breath, she blesses the thread with three great gales of her sweet-sour exhale.

The Cailleach at the end of the world then presses herself up off the cave floor, rises to the loom and settles onto her stool. Once seated, her ancient body floods with muscle memory and with a spark in her eye she begins to weave again. Down and in, under and through.

Gad, Wisconsin

Gad, Wisconsin

more-than-humans:[i]

cow, pollywog, swallow, bear, snake, kildeer, ostrich fern, daisy and red granite

playlist:

Lawrence Welk, WIGM FM, polka music, cows lowing, *She's a Rainbow* by the Rolling Stones, *Canned Goods* by Greg Brown, wind blowing in the white pines, Grandma singing while she works

libations:

milk, whisky old fashioned, coffee, Miller Genuine Draft, well water

nibbles:

cheese curds, pickles, deviled eggs, aged Gad cheddar, radishes, boiled dinner

stories:

Tatterhood, the day Grandpa saved the farmer's son from across the road from being trampled by bolting cows, *Truck* by Michael Perry, first waltz with Jimmy Gilles, age six in the Gad dance hall

Pole Star

I see you everywhere, in the stars, in the river,
to me you're everything that exists; the reality of everything.

– Virginia Woolf, Night and Day

B ack to back with earth. Crown of her head facing north, lying on the damp July grass in her grandparents' yard. In this twilight she is 10. Porous with curiosity and innocence, though much has been broken.

Overhead the wind churns, white pine needles conducting their gentle tree music into the shells of her ears. Breathing in, the perfume of clover and the tang of cow manure enters along with the blue twilight. Breathing out, she softens. Becomes still, listening.

From the house: swelling laughter, the shuffle of cards, the crack of a beer can opening flows out to her. She smiles, hearing the clatter of hand-dried dishes being set back into cupboards, and the whine of beagles as their supper of kibble, gravy, and pot roast scraps is set down. She knows the white tips of their tails will be hoisted and wagging furiously. Across the red granite gravel road, she hears the lowing of cows in Mr. Gallistel's barn.

A surge of being at home, of an unspoken knowing of place, of north, hums through her veins, raising goose bumps on her skin.

Gazing into the indigo country sky, her pupils dilate, and more light comes in. She greets star by glinting star as they present themselves; every star singing its singular strange melody. Her body opens. And softens.

Decades later she would hear stories that movement inside a star creates a vibration similar to a musical instrument. The bigger the star, the deeper the pitch.

There is one star she knows by name and, eyes wide with wonder, her gaze settles upon this pulsing pinprick of light. She knows this guiding star, Polaris. She knows this northern pole star is part of the Little Dipper, Ursa Minor, the little bear. Polaris is a compass for those lost. At sea and on land.

From Polaris, her gaze softens, taking in the expanse of sky. Each and every star a solar miracle, a story made of stories, telling stories. With the universe in her ears she knows that there are things she will never have words for.

Her eyes breathe in

Her heart breathes out

Her spine breathes in

Her feet breathe out

The grass breathes in

The soil breathes out

The sky breathes in

The stars breath out

Suspended between the Great Below and

the Great Above she listens. She sees.

For an incandescent moment and yet for all times, she sees every star, even those hidden in the folds of deep space. The light of every star lit luminous, pulsing, utterly alive pours into her hazel eyes.

Jaw slack, eyes wide, her head ringing with a love of the stars,[ii] she sees she is all that light and knows in that moment her place in a miraculous world.

Waning Gibbous Moon in Pisces

I 'm here. I'm here. I am here. In Gad. I left Dad's apartment on Monday. His apartment is clean and empty. I did it! What a ride. All of his possessions have been thrown, sold, given to charity, or are now here with me at Grandma and Grandpa's.

Fuck, I need to rest, regroup, restore. My body is exhausted.

I am here—in Gad. I don't have to go back to the suburbs ever again! Outside my window, I can hear the wind in the white pines and the cows mooing. So soothing! Downstairs I can smell and hear Grandma making supper—walleye. Massive exhale.

I've been in the deep end too long and haven't had a moment to sit and breathe and write.

Feeling numb. Too much in me to process right now though writing helps.

My dad is dead. His body is ash. At his memorial service, his brother who sexually abused me showed up—totally uninvited—and I am carrying that moment where he looked into my eyes and saw that I knew.

And Venus is dead; she was the most amazing cat I've ever known. I can't believe it's been five months. I am struggling to process that. I can't even think about it, it hurts too much. So much to process, breath by breath, day by day.

I'm going to hang here for a week or so and then head to Mercer, north and east, to housesit for a friend. Some serious rest and release can happen there.

This weekend I'm driving up to Springbrook, to Mike's place. Mike, who I met through my online search for a pen pal. It will be the first time I've visited his cabin in the north woods. He's been a godsend the past month, coming down to Milwaukee multiple times helping haul Dad's stuff and even more importantly, to play and laugh and love, and be in our bodies together. So good to be held and seen. So grateful for this shared love of Lake Superior. It's been three months since I met the mighty Big Momma Lake along the South Shore, and I fell ass over tea kettle in love with that massive inland sea.

That moment driving north from Gad, from Milwaukee, from the crucible of Dad's end of life dance, I felt her from 30 miles away. She is magnificent. She led me to Mike. I am so grateful for this connection with Mother Superior.

Often, especially when I'm struggling. I think about the Lake, recalling that presence, knowing *that* lives in me. Lake Superior offers me meaning, a connection to something larger than my life drama playing out. I can't wait to be with her again.

Anyway, on Saturday I'll head closer to her and to Mike's for a Halloween Dance—it's a contra dance and the band *Duck for the Oyster* is playing. I think it's the same band that played at Michael Perry's wedding. I've really gotten into his books *Truck* and *Coop* these past few months! I've been working on a costume in between the madness of clearing Dad's apartment, and I've pulled together all the right pieces.

Samantha gave me a red mask she made. I have an orange scarf, a yellow top, a funky green resale belt, a long, sparkly blue skirt with electric blue tights I bought in Edinburgh years ago, and I completely covered my pair of tall boots with purple glitter. Yes, I shall be a rainbow. Totally makes sense, it has been a year of intense rain and shine. I haven't told Mike yet and I don't know what he's going as. We'll surprise each other. I have that butterfly feeling in my belly when I think about Mike. Not sure what's going to happen there. Time will tell.

Other than dancing my ass off with Mike this Saturday and housesitting in Mercer, I don't know much about my future. I'm not even sure I'll go back to Iowa. I just don't know. I need to get quiet and still, meditate, and soak in the rural night sky, tromp through the forest, and be with nature, and then, maybe, I will know what's next. I might have to go up to Lake Superior too, and soon. I can't believe it took me 44 years to find my way there. I am so smitten with that place. Along her shores, I feel things I haven't felt since Scotland. What if I found a place that feels as right, as wild, magnificent, and profound as Scotland, and rather than thousands of miles away, from Gad, and Grandma and Grandpa, this place, this lake was like 100 miles or less away. What if?

Holy shit, my life is a mess. I'm going to walk on my road, my beloved red granite, dead-end gravel road. That always helps.

I see a way forward. I feel both weary and curious. I know I'll be okay.

Protection

Down the red granite gravel road to a cul-du-sac of
white birch, white pine, open to the Divine.

Ice cream pails tied snug to our waists, old scarves
wrapped 'round to our heads.

Meaty deerflies roved on thick wings as we three; Grandma,
Grandpa, and me pressed into the raspberry's sweet-sharp weave.

In silence we picked while the air hummed heavy with humidity,
holding us close, breathing in sync, fingers stained
red with berry blood.

There in the mass of matted thorn, Grandpa said one word, *Bear.*
Here, only heartbeats ago, snout and paw, teeth and tongue,
stained red with berry blood.

Waning Gibbous Moon in Gemini

F ewer than two weeks ago, I left Dad's apartment and suburbia for the last time with his security deposit and last month's rent check in my back pocket. I had a plan. At that time, I was soaring with a deep sense of accomplishment and drowning in fumes of exhaustion. The plan then had been to layover in Gad with Grandma and Grandpa for a week. Soak up some of Grandma's home cooking, take long hot baths in honest-to-god clean well water, listen to the white pines sing to me, as they always had, and begin digesting this intense end of life experience with him.

Gad time would be just a wayside before heading north and east to the woods near Mercer, to housesit through November. There, I could begin to rest and digest. After Mercer, I wasn't sure. There was a part of me that was keen to go back to my life in Fairfield, Iowa. Back to the big, vaulted sky of the prairie lands and to a community of 3000+ meditators, like me. That was two weeks ago.

Now everything is off the map.

Six days ago, on Halloween, I drove north to Springbrook from Gad. I slipped into my lover's arms for an All Hallow's Eve contra dance with *Duck for the Oyster*. That night Mike and I were humming with hot, fresh promise. What a night. The best and the most fucked-up night ever.

Time stopped on many levels that night at 12:43 a.m. on November first, when Mike's heart stopped. We were in bed. We were just falling asleep. We were falling in love.

Now there is no plan.

Since that night, that dance, the days and nights have been one long in-between space of shock and sobbing. An unknown netherland of such psychic pain that I actually had the desire to pick up a knife and cut myself. I wanted to. But I didn't. I wanted to hurt on the outside as much as I hurt on the inside.

I am in shock.

Waning Gibbous Moon in Cancer

I 've started going to therapy in Wausau with a very wise, conscious, and compassionate woman. Feeling extremely grateful for her. After hearing my story and the events of the past eight month, after asking some questions and taking in my answers, she offered, "I think you are having a spiritual initiation." Hearing those words was so helpful even though I'm not sure what that means.

She said, "It is possible that since you experienced early childhood sexual abuse, any existing trauma in your body may be triggered by your more recent experiences."

She said, "Now is a time to deeply tend to yourself."

She said, "I'm glad you are here."

I felt some strange reassurance in her words that my body was responding the way bodies do to traumatic events, old ones and new ones. An old wound has been reopened and now is a time of initiation. I am indeed off the map and into the unplanned journey.

Here in the crucible of my life, through these experiences I'm aware of becoming more vast; my story becoming larger. I am feeling all the horrible feelings that this life rupture created. Choosing to see this through a larger lens, as a spiritual initiation (which humans have chosen and resisted for thousands of years) gives me strange hope that at some point in time I will come out the other side of the pain and intensity and there I will meet another newer, wiser layer of myself. I guess we shall see.

I feel a terrible, beautiful, inexplicable vastness in me.

JOURNAL | NOVEMBER 8 2009, GAD, WISCONSIN

Waning Gibbous Moon in Leo

Three weeks ago, I arrived with everything I had while living with Dad. A carload of clothes, food, and books. Now all that still sits, a heaping island on the floor of Grandpa's office beneath a bumper sticker affixed to the wall that reads, *A Farmer is Outstanding in His Field.* Slowly I am taking stuff upstairs to my room.

Yesterday, as I carried an armful up the stairs, a red and white sandstone rock tumbled out. It was about the size of a fist and heart-shaped. I picked it up feeling the coolness and deep time in my hand. I didn't recognize it.

Mike was many things: traveler, lover of lakes—the colder the better—dancer, and hunter. He was also heart rock man. During our blink-of-an-eyelash courtship, they spilled from his pockets, back-packs, and, it seemed like, thin air. He offered me many along with his bright, beating, northern heart.

While living with Dad, a few rocks had found their way into my world, reminders to ground, be still. Most were from Lake Michigan, collected along the shore at the Schlitz Audubon Center. They were set on makeshift altars, tucked into pockets, placed on the kitchen counter, and used to crush fresh thyme. Then there were a precious few that Mike gave me. This rock that had just tumbled out was from neither category. This rock, that fits perfectly into my palm, is a mystery. Maybe Mike tucked it in somewhere. My heart swelled at this realization, and I let the tears fall.

Later on, I went for a walk down my road; two blessed miles of red granite that dead ends into a wild tangle of forest. I have been walking, skipping, and trotting along Gad Road since I was old enough to trot. This road and the pasture, forest of popple and maple, spruce and ash, and marshland that it moves through, are as known to me as my own hands. I've watched these trees grow and they have watched me. This road is my therapy and now even more so. This road is now the only place I can fully howl out my grief. Where I can sob until I'm blessed in salt tears and snot.

So there I was bellowing this bright pain to a near-naked maple, to the ceaseless swaying popple, moving trance-like over the red gravel lost in shock and denial.

I am so deep down the rabbit hole of shock. It is a continent.

My body felt like a truckload of crushed gravel. Heavy. Crunched. So heavy; my heart, my blood, my bones. As my feet shuffled the rest of my body forward along the road, I prayed and prayed. I wept and prayed. I howled and prayed. I prayed to the spruce, the cedar, to anyone, to Mike, God, Divine Mother. I prayed for one ridiculous thing: *how could I connect with Mike in some way. How?*

It seems strange but deep inside I sensed that Mike wanted and was trying to connect with me. I could and can feel him, maddeningly just beyond the reach of my five senses.

My shoes kicked a spray of gravel and a little tan and pink granite heart rock scuttled out in front of me. I picked it up. I tucked its coolness into my palm, feeling sad and then grateful. It felt like a little communication, just a little answer to my prayer saying, *Yes. I'm here.*

I feel him.

Waning Crescent Moon in Leo

L ike me, Mike loved the bagpipes. Sometime just after my dad's passing, he sent me two CDs: the *Waking Ned Devine* soundtrack, and a mix of his favorite instrumental pipe tunes, including *Amazing Grace*. He loved the film *Waking Ned Devine*. We had added watching it to the ever-growing list of things we'd do together one day. On the *Ned Devine* CD, he'd written, *the pipes on track 11 take me away*. The name of that track is *An Angel Will Cry*.

He'd sent the music because we both loved the bagpipes, and also because in early October, I was looking for some bagpipe music to play at Dad's celebration of life ceremony. I didn't play any of the songs Mike sent at the ceremony, instead I played the one song Dad requested, *Mull of Kintyre* by Paul McCartney.

It is ironic and heart crushing that I did end up playing that track, number 11, *An Angel Will Cry*, last Saturday at Mike's funeral just a few weeks after he'd sent it.

Now I'm sitting at the coffee shop in Medford, buzzing, and not just from caffeine. I have been coming here almost every day to get out of the four walls of my room at my grandparents' for a decent cup of tea, internet, and connection to the wider world. They play a satellite radio station with surprisingly eclectic music. Sara the owner has a smile that lights up the world. I need these things now.

Ten minutes ago, I was typing out an email when I heard bagpipes playing from the speakers, a rare sound coming from any music station in this part of the world.

My ears perked up and I heard Peter Gabriel's sweet voice. "Whatever fear invents I swear it makes no sense. I reach out through the border fence come down, come talk to me." I didn't recognize the song and asked Sara if she knew the name. She climbed up on a table to look at the receiver display, calling down, "It's Peter Gabriel and the song is, *Come Talk to Me.*"

Goosebumps rose on my arms. It felt like another message. I know I'm still in shock. I know that my body experienced trauma and I am heavily under that influence. I also know that I'm in a liminal space (and have been for some time with Dad's end of life dance), and a spiritual initiation that opened its wide maw the moment Mike took his last breath. And I know there's so much more than consensual reality. I know too I really, really want to connect with him. Somehow.

I am now fully covered in goosebumps—like a rash! I've just read all the lyrics, online. It's from the album, *Us.* (!!!!)

I am soaking in this ... this, whatever the fuck it is, this gorgeous balm of synchronicity, and connection, and maybe madness.

I know mystery.

Waning Crescent Moon in Libra

Dear Circle of Friends,

Thank you for receiving this email update, here in the deep end of life. Last Wednesday I went to Hayward for Mike's funeral. I stayed with his dear friends, John and Ginger, both amazing people who loved Mike very much. At the funeral I met his son Ruairi, daughter Erin, his brothers, sisters, and his father Patrick. Mike was from a big Irish family. This was the first time meeting his people. I had heard lots about them, so they were kind of familiar. Many of them had heard about me, which made it seem less surreal.

This past week has been such strange brew of tears, an almost giddy and inexplicable joy, hopelessness, and a numb nothingness. As I drove to the funeral from Gad, I saw many bald eagles. One circled over my car. I swear I am seeing them everywhere in the last week. I am so grateful for these connections with eagle. It feels like a good sign. I like it when I can tell they are checking me out. Something super beautiful about being in the sight of something so wild. I crave these wilder, *more-than-human* connections.

At the funeral I read *The Stolen Child* by W.B. Yeats. Mike loved Yeats. Plenty of tears flowed. I heard so many stories about him and learned more about his journey as a recovering alcoholic. He'd made some huge changes to his life. I learned that he loved to jump into cold water: Lake Superior, Galway Bay, any random river or lake—in all seasons. After I got back to Gad from the funeral I reached out to my dear friend, intuitive, and wise woman to share my experience. Cielle Backstrom has been a huge ally throughout the journey with Dad. These are some rich words she shared with me. It feels important to share them here, with you all. Thank you for receiving this.

It's interesting that you have been collecting stories to share for years, and now you are living in the midst of a most profound story of your own. You implied that at this point your ability to verbally express the story is still nebulous, but the picture you sketched for me is quite phenomenal, and I hope that someday you will be able to write it and share it, if you feel to do so.

As I mentioned, the image that comes to me, when you spoke of everything coming full circle, is the image of the serpent swallowing its own tail. I was thinking more about it, and how you were saying that you shared your whole background with Mike, and that he didn't share his with you, and it makes sense, really, for the progression of the circle. Do you know what I mean? It seems to me that it was up to you to be the one to come forward to complete the circle, if he would have come "forward," it may have pushed you back, and therefore the circle wouldn't have been able to close.

Here is my impression:

So, you came forward, opened completely, the circle closed, and Mike's light had fulfilled its mission, and was able to ascend. And maybe it was a healing not only for you and Mike, but perhaps you served as divine archetypes, and your experience together was assisting in a universal healing of the collective consciousness. A truly divine event. And part of you is still open, will always be open, the part that never closes, the circle is still complete, yet the humanness of your physiology is not quite ready for the immensely blown open divinity of the experience, so you have been sent spiraling into another forming circle, like ripples on the water, circles within circles, divine geometry.

Another thing that is so interesting and mythological about all this is that the closing and fusing of the circle took place on All Hallows Eve. And you were a Rainbow! Your heart was open, all your chakras were probably open and enlivened and spinning. You were a pure rainbow energy body! And when you think of all the things a rainbow symbolizes, it's pretty amazing.

This is such a beautiful understanding.

I'm still in awe and so much pain. I have so much gratitude for you all, and even my (unemotive Lutheran) family have stuck by me, accepting me as I grieve and heal, even if I'm hysterical. For the most part, they are meeting me where I'm at, rather than where they'd like me to be. For the most part.

I am still in shock and it is just sooooo fricking much. I am noticing sweet, small waves of grace that fill me from time to time. I'm praying for more of these; please do the same. The grace, when I open to it or it reveals itself, helps me hear/know/feel the bigger story, the more expansive one.

I feel like I'm on the edge and I need to either drop the body or drop the ego/mind/illusion. I need to accept this and only this, EVERYTHING in life in transitory. The thing is, I can't wish myself out of my humanness and into spirit-ness, so the grace is like the expansion, the balm inside the contraction, inside this crucible.

I feel gratitude for each of you in this wild journey.

Much love!
Tracy

Waning Crescent Moon in Sagittarius

It's been six weeks. I rest, I eat, I cry, I play cribbage, I walk the road, I find heart rocks everywhere.

A few weeks ago, a friend recommended I try some automatic writing with Mike, and hopefully receive messages back from him, from the *other* side. Sounds a little corny to even write it down and whether or not there have been actually communications with him (I still feel it was him that sent me the Peter Gabriel song!), it has been helpful. This is a little bit mad (as in crazy) ahhhh well, it seems allowed and understandable I guess, but what the fuck do I know? I know/feel that writing like this is a place to put my energy that helps me move through some of the powerlessness I feel and I do feel closer to him, I feel him in the words that seem to come from him:

12/1/09 Dear Tracita, I am here. Not sure what to say, I love you. I can hear you, feel you, keep writing, keep talking to me. I didn't want to leave, it was time, I'm still unsure, I wish I could be there with you. Don't cry. Breathe.

Just know that I am here. Always remember that. You're my Tracita and I'm

your Miquel. This is part of your story now, just like our day flying the but-

terfly kite along Lake Michigan, just like that dance, that waltz in Shell Lake.

I'm so sorry I left you. Oh God. I couldn't believe it. I still can't. You're okay—

just stay close, stay open. Breathe. I can't see the future from here but I can

feel things—just keep listening, watching and paying attention. You weren't

my first love, though you were my last—it was so deep and rich and fulfilling

to fall in love with you. God you have a beautiful heart. I know you're strug-

gling. I know what you went through with your dad was hard. I just wanted

to hold and cherish you, and wipe all of it away. The timing was perfect, in

that way, and yet it was too short. Way too short. Sweet, sweet Tracita, I am

holding you too tight ...

There's lots more of those writings between us—what a fucking trip.

In late November, I went to Lake Superior. I hiked Meyer's Creek Trail. I wept, and howled, and listened. I carved M.S + T.C. gently into the silver of a birch tree and I placed menstrual blood hearts on the birch trees too. I don't have time to write about that now, it was sublime. I'll stay with my grandparents here in Gad until early January.

There is a little cabin up north I'm going to rent. It's very rustic. No running water. No heat source other than the wood stove. I have never chopped wood before, though I do have Dad's axe. It's about five miles outside of Washburn and Lake Superior. If I'm able to be excited about anything right now, I am excited about this. The rest of my family thinks I'm nuts.

One day, I shall tell this story, as storytellers do, not only for my sake but for those who have dropped into the nether-world of grief, who have lived through their dark nights of the soul and for those who have stories of their own that they are burning to tell.

Grandma is helping me sew a quilt. Oxblood maroon and ochre, holy colors. We bake and cook together. Mostly I feel a bit out of it, she's always patient and kind. The three of us play a lot of cribbage, and I pretty much lose all the time. I've been praying despite their age (89!) and many health issues, that they stick around for a while. I couldn't bear losing them anytime soon, though it is inevitable. *Memento Mori.*

I hear the north calling me.

Golden

It takes two to speak the truth—one to speak and another to hear.

– Henry David Thoreau

I am healing. It's been four years since my dad and Mike's deaths and now here in Gad, the tender, brutal, and beautiful threshold of death opens again.

In August, in the threshold of Lughnasa, the apples cling, thick and sweet, to the gnarled tree while yellow finches spill like golden coins from the branches. At every age and chapter I have known this tree, felt favored by her petals. I have climbed and twined up into her branches, sat well-fed in her shade breathing in her ripe perfume.

Between the well-known, well-worn house and the apple trees stand two white pine giants. Their needles cascade like plush curtains framing the house. These too are old, dear friends. Their tenant sparrows wake us at dawn, their wind-laced lullabies ferry us to sleep. Inside the white house my grandparents dwell, their home of 69 years. I am here even when I am not.

Now, my grandma, the beloved Grand Mother of my heart who rarely slows down from tending to the warp and weft of her family and household, has stopped. She sleeps on the sofa as the stories of her lifetime spark in her mind one last time before ebbing back into the story behind all stories.

She is dying. Leona Anne Dassow Albrecht, almost 93, is shedding her body. Her tremendous north-dwelling heart, that faithful old pump, has seen her through nearly 73 years of marriage, five births, a score of deaths and thousands of jars of pickles. Her purposeful hands that kneaded infinite loaves are paper-thin, warm, and unspeakably soft on my cheek.

Fifty years of memories vie for my attention. Grandma and the weaving of her full and fruitful life; cooking spareribs and sauerkraut, baking raspberry kuchen, canning beans, hanging laundry out to dry, sewing quilts, and being available in every way to whoever needed her.

My grandma animated her bones for 33,919 days, inhaling and exhaling, going about her near lifetime role as homemaker, baking and sewing, all the while singing in her always high, always old lady, always off-key grandma voice, *Oh my darling, oh my darling, oh my darling Clementine. You are lost and gone forever, dreadful sorry Clementine ...*

She is of *this* place here in Northcentral Wisconsin—Gad, in the township of Bern, halfway down a dead end, red granite, gravel road, on the cusp of Taylor and Marathon counties, six miles from Medford. My grandparents moved here with their growing family from above their small cheese factory a few pastures away in 1950 and the view in all directions has changed little since then.

To the north, where, at the T of Gad and Willow Roads, I drove into the ditch in a snowstorm when I was 20 years old, from there a 120 mile patchwork of pasture and forest eventually kisses the Big Lake, Superior. Out the back door and into the east lies their garden bed of radishes, kohlrabi, and carrots where I first learned about planting, watering, and harvesting. The garden leads to pasture, which opens into the tangle of birch, pine, and ash. South along the road, yarrow, daisy, milkweed, and clover trail into the forest of birch, pine, maple, and spruce I've watched grow over 47 years. Across the road to the west, the barn built by Anton Gallistel is still the highest building in sight and, where every summer of my childhood, I milked cows and played hide and seek in the hay mow. Every direction inevitably leads into forest where raven flies with her prize along the tree line, where mother bear lumbers nose to earth, and above, great hordes of stars spill a milk path across the wide sky.

Leona, the ninth of thirteen children, all of whom she outlived, spoke only German until she went to school at the age of five and her last year of school was eighth grade. During a game of cribbage, if something didn't go her way she used a phrase, *Holy Shmutzenfink*, her personal swear word.

Now, 92 years into her story, she lies at this next threshold. Visitors from five counties stop in for closure and peace. Some eyes remain dry. Some eyes meet her blue eyes with even, steady love. Those eyes that cannot meet hers speak in the hushed language of the heart. It is a time where even the most stoic of the bunch (and there are many) relinquish I love yous like fat summer raindrops that can't be stopped.

For the visitors, I bake sugar cookies using her mother Magdalena's recipe. I offer her a piece and she takes it into her mouth, chews and swallows carefully, then licking honeyed crumbs from her dry lips says, *They're good*. This will be the final feast, the last solid food she'll take to her singing mouth. My grandpa, in his recliner, watches without speech. Daily he sits beside her for a spell, eyes rimmed crimson, burning to spill the tears.

At night, between sleep and dreaming, I lie awake feeling the momentousness of this time, here with her and Grandpa. I notice this strange, grateful acceptance of the challenging events of the last four years: my dad's cancer, Mike's death, choosing to move to the Big Lake, to chop wood and carry water here in Wisconsin. All my life, I have come back here again and again, over and over, weaving in and out of every season, every chapter of my life, soaking in Gad and their love. I weep hot, hot tears for what will be lost, when Grandma goes, when Grandpa dies.

At night, I lie listening to her breathe, tuning in for the final cycle. The nights are all restlessness and old shadows. I soothe her by climbing into her bed, hip to hip, singing *You are my sunshine, my only sunshine. You make me happy when skies are gray. You'll never know, dear, how much I love you. Please don't take my sunshine away* ...

I breathe her in. We pray, *Our Father who art in heaven,* and I wet her dry lips with a sponge. We are deep in threshold time now. All six senses are lit more luminous.

One golden afternoon as she sleeps, I sit beside her watching the too-bold August sun press through the window. She stirs. Her eyes open, fluttering like moths. She sits up and raises her arms high.

Her eyes widen and she calls out, *Ma!* Then, *Mother.*

She opens were arms wider still. Moments stretch. My breath held. The clock on the wall ticking. She says, *Oh, I love you. I love you all,* her smile as wide as a sunset. Her eyes electric. Her ancestors no longer at her back but before her. Her beloveds, her lineage of deep country farming folk, Hildegard, Ray, Bertha, Gertie, Bill, Alma, Elsie, Les, all 13 of them. All her siblings and her Ma and Pa.

Again time slows to a near halt.

Then, she turns to look directly into me. Her eyes lit with some inner fire. A dawning recognition lights her face and in awe she slowly says to me, *It's just a play. It's just a show.*

It's just a play. It's just a show.

I am searching her eyes and they are filled with a truth I have never seen there. Time stops. The house is so still, as if it is taking this in too. Then this liminal spell is broken by a door slamming somewhere.

She settles back onto the pillows. Her eyes droop, the veil closes as this sublime clarity ebbs. What follows then is a flickering string of speechless moments as I lay my head on her shoulder breathing in sync with her.

For the next week, all spoken language would ebb from her as she moved closer and closer to that place where we all shall meet. She still smelled like my grandma; of clover and milk, flour and sunshine, fried potatoes, and aqua net.

Then at noon on the sixth of August, her soft presence became too big for her body and out she slipped into the Everything. We were fortunate to have her to ourselves for a few hours, as unorthodox as it was. I'd insisted.

I bathed her creased, soft as satin, pale as the moon skin. Each line a story.

Utterly humbled, unspeakably honored to tend to my grandmother in this way.

A deep peace and silence hung in the air. Grandpa watched from his recliner which, like him, had seen better days. Each caress of the warm water with rose oil was a blessing. Blessing her belly/womb that held and birthed five lives, blessing her umbilical connection to her mother Magdalena who gave birth to 15. Blessing her hands that soothed and kneaded, her arms that hung out thousands of pieces of clean clothes to dry on the line, her singing throat, her polka-dancing feet.

Grandpa watched this holy act, eyes seeping. The low rumble of his voice slipped into that space to thank me. And *thanks* wasn't a common word to fall from those stubborn and stoic lips. I dressed her in something colorful and comfortable and gathered flowers and plants from her garden; spiderwort for the weaving yet to come, rose for the love she was, clover for the farming of her childhood, and white pine for the songs they held, and placed them around her head. When she was ready we all gathered: her husband, her children, and some of her grandchildren. Then we raised our voices true and clear, singing *Amazing Grace* until even the flies on the ceiling were on their knees.

Outside the August sun baked the red granite road, the white pines whispered their wind-song lullabies, and the perfume of untasted apples spilled in through the window.

Four Generation
Sugar Cookie Recipe

Mix

3 egg yokes

1 Cup shortening (butter is best)

1 Cup sugar

Add

4 Tablespoons milk

¼ Teaspoon salt

1 Teaspoon baking powder

3 Cups flour

1 Teaspoon baking soda

Chill–Roll–Bake

Cut out with cookie cutter, or 2-3 inch glass rimmed with sugar

Bake @ 350 degrees F.

Let cool and frost.

Variations

Great Grandma Magdalena's: add 1 Teaspoon anise seed.

Grandma Leona's: as is above.

Mom's (Lorna): add 1 Teaspoon vanilla.

Mine: add 1 Teaspoon vanilla and 1 Teaspoon cardamom.

The Well of Grief

Grief, the tiger that devours,

The strawberry that feeds,

The oven that bakes,

The ice that melts,

The bread that feeds.

Grief, the spell that casts,

The stone that skips,

The wound that bleeds,

The river that carries,

The raven that devours .

Grief, the spark that ignites

The avalanche that buries,

The wolf that kills,

The ring that weds,

The lover that ravishes.

Verklempt

Travelers, it is late.

Life's sun is going to set.

During these brief days that you have strength,

be quick and spare no effort of your wings.

– Jalal ad-Din Muhammad Rumi

I n the aftermath of Grandma's death there were no cookies left in the cookie jar. No bread was baked. No Greible soup made. No beef roast. Or gravy. Or mashed potatoes peeled by her hands.

There was ham. She wanted ham for her funeral luncheon. Grandma loved a good piece of pork. After her funeral, there was plenty of ham. We ate her ham like a sacrament. Then we froze the rest.

My grandma refused to have a pacemaker put in. She said she was ready. It took her two weeks. She left her body on the sixth of August. Not the fourth —that was her 73rd wedding anniversary. Not the fifth, that was my 48th birthday but on the sixth, her very own death day.

Sympathy cards filled the mailbox. They stacked up like pancakes on the dining room table. In the hot afternoons, I would make lunch for Grandpa; maybe leftovers, maybe pan-fried walleye from my uncles' recent fishing trip to Canada. After lunch, maybe we'd play a game or two of cribbage. Eventually, like the sun seeks the western horizon, he would return to his reclining chair that smelled of urine to nap. My grandpa knew how to work and he knew how to nap.

Some days I would ask him if he wanted me to read sympathy cards. If he gave me the nod, I would pull out five or six and read. These days, his eyes always looked red and sore, like they were burning to cry. As I read, sometimes tears squeezed out leaving polka dots on his dark shirt. Sometimes he chuckled at a kindly written note, perhaps detailing a memory of his wife, and of him, and sometimes he'd elaborate—eyes a hundred years away.

He took in every kind word written in those cards, let every heart-felt condolence sink into his crusty, quadruple bypassed ol' heart. So did I. Those were poignant days in the aftermath without her singing rising up from the stove. Without her, their home place of 72 years was something other. Together, Grandpa and I were broken open in her absence. While we read the cards, crying and laughing and soaking in the ocean of it all, my mom—their daughter Lorna—took her grief to the garden to pull weeds.

~

Two weeks after my grandma's funeral Grandpa had a doctor appointment in town, and I would take him. He came out of their bedroom which was still furnished with the bedframe and drawers they'd had all their married life. They were good at tending things. Making them last. As Grandpa came out of the bedroom, he was trying to fit his stout body into a light blue denim button-down shirt, worn with age. I offered to help, and he let me. I got one arm in. Then the other. It was a tight fit.

Then I saw that embroidered on the top front of the shirt was a zebra and a giraffe. I thought, *this is Grandma's shirt.* I thought, *does he know he's been trying to stuff himself into her shirt?* At 92 you never know. Before I thought more about it, it slipped out, softly, "This looks like Grandma's shirt." He gave a little grunt and a nod and then I got it. I said, "There, it looks nice," as I buttoned him in. In that moment, I felt the little boy in him, the one who lost his mother, Laura, to tuberculosis when he was four.

I said no more though my throat closed tight—verklempt. Tears pooled in my eyes, fell and dotted on his shoulder. I rubbed his back a bit and said, "Well, we better be going." He stood up and grabbed his walker. Well-swaddled, and as close as he could get to his beloved, we headed to town.

~

Two weeks later, on the 9th of September, just a month after Grandma's funeral, we finally finished the last of her funeral ham for supper. That night I'd made a chocolate cake, Grandpa's favorite. The next day he was scheduled to begin chemotherapy to treat a recently-detected, persistently growing cancer. Yes, at nearly 93, the medical powers-that-be offered him this and he took it. He chose it and we all knew the chemo would be the death of him. His choice. Ever the fighter.

The next morning, I found him alongside his bed, their bed. That morning it was his turn to make the Great Journey. I sat with his still-warm body.

A bit later I walked upstairs to my mom's bedroom, waking her gently, so gently from sleep to tell her.

"Mumma, Grandpa is dead."

Later three of his four sons, his only daughter, and a handful of his grandchildren, gathered around his body. I dressed him in Grandma's giraffe shirt (no-one but me noticed) and wreathed his head with apple branches and boughs of white pine. We sang *Amazing Grace* and *Home on the Range*.

Thus began our farewell to Lorin Arthur Albrecht—cheesemaker, WWII vet, and lifelong fisherman—as he left this place for the next. The son of Laura and Arthur, father of five, grandfather of 15 and the world's most bullheaded, salt of the earth, son of Gad there ever was.

On Gad Road

This road holds the layers of many lives
One of them my own.
In the layers, walking
there are ghosts at my back.
Land Ancestors—Oceti Sakowin,
Menomonie, Anishinaabe knowing.
Language lost in the fecund marsh maw,
Found in spangled popple's cry—
Old stories of sky.
A whole people's remembering.
Now the grief song wails
Through the woods
From my lips.

Offer a full plate.

In the layers, walking
there are ghosts at my back.
Great Grandma's weary womb,
Great Grandpa's grief-trapped hands,
Grandpa's sun-kissed face,
Grandma's berry picking song.
My heart is full,
This tribe is scattered.

Offer a full glass.

In the layers walking
there are ghosts at my back.

Tiny, calloused feet running, red granite spraying,
Dervish dancing, daisy picking, ice cream pail
Brimming with pollywogs
Who will never grow legs.

I am many lives.

Maiden
Mother to none
Becoming crone.

Offer a full song.

Dreamers, lovers, disbelievers—what do you say?
Come, be the walker!
Walk the layers of your own gravel road.
Honor the ancestors at your back.
Make love with your life,

Sing your full story
Back to the layers.

– a nod to Stanley Kunitz's The Layers

Lake Superior

Lake Superior

more-than-humans:

eagle, raven, coyote, birch, lupine, fiddlehead fern, Four Mile
Creek, the Lake, red sandstone

playlist:

Silence, WOJB FM, Across the Universe by The Beatles, falling snow,
melting snow, Cory Chisel, The Pines, Peter Gabriel's album *Us*,
crackling of a wood fire

libations:

well and local artesian water, Earl Grey Tea, Talisker

nibbles:

lake trout, popcorn, blueberries, birch syrup, oatmeal

stories:

The Handless Maiden, the butterfly who hatched in the cabin
one January night while I watched Mike's favorite film; *Waking
Ned Devine*

Waning Crescent Moon in Cancer

h ello. I've recently chosen to relocate to the Milwaukee area to support my father who is dying of lung cancer. I am missing the deep peace and wildness of the north woods (have family in Gad, near Medford). In June I had a short visit to Lake Superior and I can't stop thinking about the Lake and what I felt when I was there. I thought it might be nice to connect with someone who knew this Great Lake, perhaps as a pen pal and maybe in person when I can get away. Not looking for casual sex ever or a long-term relationship. Just a pen pal. I am well into middle age. I meditate, exercise, love nature and art, and aspire to live simply. Although I grew up in the Milwaukee area, I am truly a fish out of water in the burbs/big city and I am making the best of an intense and at times uncomfortable situation. The ideal pen pal would have a love of Lake Superior and a sense of humor and adventure. I look forward to hearing from you.

Hi,

I read your post on Craigslist and understand. I just thought I'd send you a note of encouragement! I know, from past experience, how difficult this time will be for you. I too put my life on hold for my dying mother. After all is said and done, I would do it all again in a heartbeat. You will never regret your undertaking. I live an hour south of Lake Superior, in the woods near Hayward. I have known the lake all my life. She is mighty, mighty!

I'm not looking for anything from you, and I wanted to let you know that I'm around, should you need someone to yell at. Let me know if you want to be penpals.

– Mike

Be A Great Sea

*There is a basin in the mind where words float around on thought
and thought on sound and sight. Then there is a depth of thought untouched
by words, and deeper still a gulf of formless feelings untouched by thought.* [iii]

– Zora Neale Hurston, Their Eyes Were Watching God

A vast boreal forest lined the way, bold and branched, naked and snow-clad in the white lush winds of winter. In the season's repose, tree after tree after tree bristled the land: spruce, white pine, oak, birch, balsam, maple, and ash. Not the endless procession of ancients that once rooted, those 1000-year-old giants who rose into the glassy blue, before they were logged. These tall-reaching trees are their kith and kin, their wild aftermath, rolling out over 21st century Northern Wisconsin.

The North hummed in my veins:

Sentinel trees council lost laughter and grace of ghosts.
a silent sea awaits, ice shrouds fathoms down
yet deeper there is life there is water. Listen.

The North spoke. It had been speaking to me since I was an infant. *Going up north* meant a four-hour car ride to my grandparent's house in Gad. Going up north meant being in the circle of my grandma's arms, her love, her cooking: fresh bread, Greible soup, fresh cheddar from their cheese factory, and apple kuchen topped with Mauel's French Vanilla ice cream. Up north meant wild spaces, the seemingly endless sea of forest and swamp which flowed around islands of pasture, all stitched together by red granite gravel roads. North meant both wilderness and safety.

Now in this winter of epic heartbreak, the north spoke, calling me. I listened. And so north and further north I traveled on Highway 13 beneath a stone-colored sky. With a snug cargo of the utilitarian and the nourishing: books, axe, grandma-made quilts, cast iron skillets, winter wear, teacups, art, and my grandma's old, white enamel chamber pot. All this, a broken-open heart, and a nervous system laced with post-traumatic stress would occupy my new northern home.

The sleek oak-handled axe had belonged to my dad. My inheritance and a talisman to the unknown. Could I swing this axe to chop the wood I would need to heat my winter?

This would be my first winter without my dad's presence walking, sleeping, dreaming on this Earth. His life ended days before the autumn equinox. Wayne Willis Chipman was a man who danced to Taj Mahal's juicy rhythms, who delighted in frozen custard, Miles Davis and single malt. He traveled great distances for meatloaf and the quiet listening he knew in the woods. The deeper the better. His pockets were filled with stories of buckshot, hunting ducks, and late-night card games. Lusty and robust Michigan poet and novelist Jim Harrison was a god to him. From age 17 until he retired in his late fifties, he was a sheet metal worker. He followed his father—my grandpa Chips—into the trade. His hands bent and fitted the sheet metal innards of hundreds of buildings throughout Milwaukee from the Auditorium to Miller Stadium. His work/life is inextricably woven into that old-world city on Lake Michigan, his Great Lake. He lived all his 70 years in Milwaukee, always close to the lake. Lake Michigan ran in his blood; his spirit now swims in her waters.

After his death, I felt a flood of relief, for him and for myself. His six-month journey with cancer had been a long one. We had forged his uncharted end of life journey together. I was blessed to bear witness to this holy and inevitable reckoning. My dad's shadowlands were not tidy, nor peace-filled, but a messy mash of dark-marshed regrets and deep ancestral grief. Within that mix, there were also achievements, accomplishments, and more than a few wild joys. After his death, along with relief, there was a deep sense of feeling both unleashed and unprotected without his physical presence.

So, on this January day, I drove north with his iron-headed axe, perpetually red-rimmed eyes, and a black bag filled with more grief that I knew what to do with. First Venus, then my dad, and then Mike. I was heading north and off the map with questions so thick in my mind, they seemed sometimes to hunt the wind, seeking answers. And strangely there was grace or what I call grace. This larger, deeper, flowing interdependent connection that I was just a small part of. This grace, an awareness of Source, God, the Unified Field slipped in slant-wise under the blanket of the star-salted night. Or along the liminal space where sandstone met a great inland sea. There, with a lung full of indigo, at the edge of my world, the questions all fell away.

Eager and anxious, exhausted, and naïve, I was leaving a string of endings and arriving to a beginning which started with another great lake. It was the fourth of January. Mike had been gone for two months and four days. It was -14 degrees outside without the wind chill and as I pulled up to the cabin, to this new north dwelling home, I whispered a greeting to the tangle of snow-flocked trees.

All around, blue-hued, lake effect snow shrouded everything. There, set in that pure white sat the cabin: 400 square feet, 30 years old, handbuilt, and uninsulated. It had a wood stove. There was no running water. I was home.

I would soon discover that from the cabin, the trees led branch by bough out to a wide, star-gazing meadow. From there, follow the tracks made by deer, bobcat, and coyote; moving past the well, stepping into the forest and down a steep slope of cedar to a silver-ribboned creek singing wet winter music.

This creek—Four Mile Creek—flows just that far, bleeding into the largest freshwater lake in the world: Lake Superior. So large is this cold, inland sea that if all the water[iv] in ki[v] were to spill up and out, it would cover the entire continents of North and South America in a foot of water.

The Ojibwe call Lake Superior *Gichi-gami* (pronounced gitchi-gahmi). One translation means *be a great sea.*[vi] The Ojibwe ("good person") have tended and lived on this land since the late 1400s, arriving from The Great Salt Sea of the east. The Anishinaabe knew, know, and will know this lake and land in ways I can only dream of and long for. It is this longing, and some grief, that has brought me here—to know ki better.

This Great Sea, whose presence I felt so keenly from such great distance. This lake who I'd heard stories of as a child. This lake who I had only met for the first time six months before. This lake brought me to my knees, made my heart roar and croon.

Gichi-gami had become my navigator, my Polaris, my teacher and mirror, guiding me further up, further in. Further north. I had come to this boreal forest, to Gichi-gami to be near to the inexpressible wildness in my soul, and the train wreck that was my life. I had come whether I was ready or not.

That day, David, who I was renting from, met me at the cabin. He asked if I'd ever lived alone in such an isolated place.

"I have not," I said.

"Have you ever used an axe or split wood before?" He asked.

"I have not. Not yet," I said.

"Do you know how to start a fire?" He asked.

"Oh yes, I do. Sometimes many at a time." Smiling warmly but missing the meaning of my comment, he asked if I was uneasy about taking this on.

"Yes, and no." I answered truthfully.

He seemed satisfied with this and thus began my first lesson in splitting wood. I flailed and failed. I was also keen and determined. After a round of attempts, I set the axe down and we walked the 50 yards to the well at the edge of the forest.

The well, the source I would draw holy water from, who I would court like a lover—leaving offerings of cake and herring, tea and Talisker. The well, where three times a week I'd visit to fill five-gallon containers with gorgeous boreal wetness. Then I'd tow 80+ pounds of water back through feet of snow in a stalwart blue toboggan. This sacred practice wove me into the web of winter and my own life.

David and I walked, snowshoes buoying us on the powdered glass mounds of snow. Our breath hung like cold linen in the air. The copse of pine and spruce bowed and ducked in the ever-white wind. Each snowflake a droplet of water, each a winter mandala, amassing and glittering in the cold coin of the gauzy sun. These gifts and good medicine were all around: bobcat paw prints, a maze of deer tread, and crow's chuckling shadow gliding on the snow and so many more would sustain me for the next two winters.

These two winters were my time to chop wood and carry water. These two winters were my next Dark Night of the Soul, a time in which Katherine May describes in her book, *Wintering* as "*a season in the cold ... a fallow period when you are cut off from the world. A time that is usually involuntary, lonely and painful.*" Life events had brought me to my knees and I was choosing to step as consciously as I could into my wintering.

David left me to it, to my wild life, to the elements, the axe, the two cords of unsplit hardwood, to my fire tending and water carrying. As he drove away, I wouldn't blame him for wondering what in the hell he was thinking, renting me the place.

That evening I sat taking it all in, stoking the fire bright. It had been a long day, a long week. Bloody hell, it had been a long year. Three deaths, a mountain of grief and three moves in the last six months had altered me in still unfathomable ways. No translation was yet to be found. A unique new terrain was widening out before me in these wild woods.

My first night under the weight of that forest of stars I slept a dreamless sleep. Somewhere around three a.m. I woke and fed the wood stove. These middle-of-the-night fire feedings would become part of a heavy-lidded dark-of-night ritual until spring solidly arrived in May.

Sunrise squeezing through the trees woke me, and a cutting wind met me on my trot to the outhouse—another new part of my daily routine. The fire in the stove warmed me, the flames hissing out dragon tales long forgotten. Gazing out at the sun-spilled white, I knew it was time.

Layered in wool and fleece and flannel, that morning, I wed myself with wood and fire, to ice and iron. My dad always said chopping wood warms you twice. Inside I was warm with porridge and determination. Outside, the air at minus 14° F smelled indescribably sweet. Sweet with silence. Time felt fuller, more substantial as I stepped from the fire-fed warmth to the icy bright cold.

Standing over the piled cords of wood—fallen bones of decades and stories—I chose a chunk of maple as a chopping block. My hands found an opalescent limb of birch, and I set it to balance on the block. I would come to love the maddening zen-like dance of balancing rough-cut logs readying them for splitting. What could I give to show my thanks? Sage, honey, meat, a story? Would they be enough?

The axe fit well in my hands. The handle was smooth. The head was heavy. I liked the uneven weight of it. Wind stirred sunshine in the long branches. My breath rolled in and receded like waves, my heart a drum, and a mask-faced chickadee sang out. With care and intention, I stepped up to the log, coming to ground, to focus, to listen.

My attempts were awkward, comical, and unsuccessful at first. Eventually, I set down the axe and stomped around an old broad-reaching oak, listening to the swish of my feet moving through the snow before returning to my task. An oak leaf skittered along the top of the snow. Such silence. With the axe in hand, I planted my feet and brought my attention to the center of that birch log, to the pink-ringed heartwood. I considered ring after ring radiating out to the papery white bark. The rings mapped ki's precious life. There was a fleeting urge to cover up the log, protecting the vulnerability there. Red squirrel scolded from a cedar limb.

Gripping the axe between my two hands I inhaled. I lifted it up and around, swinging it overhead. My arms and the axe stretched to the zenith of my reach, sun-bound, pausing. Holding that inhale, refocusing my gaze to the inner ring I asked in a whisper, *"Will you let me cleave and disrupt the center of you? Will you give me what's left of your life?"* A sooty, squat, junco eyed me from a branch and zipped away.

Exhaling, letting the axe fall, led by gravity, by the weight of the head's heavy metal, by intention, and momentum, by a willingness to surrender to the not knowing, by the grace of ghosts and the magic of grief, by the silent lull of winter. Overhead, through the weaving tree limbs, eagle, head and tail blended into winter light, spiraled.

The axe head hit. Burying deep into the once lively core, cleaving the mother limb as two newly born split logs exploded out, landing inert in the snow.

A strong grace wrapped around me then, intimate and wild in that heart-drumming silence. The *me* of me slipped away into everything.

All the elements surrounding, engulfing, becoming. A great, inland sea.

A Tongue Too Old for Memory

The wild does not have words.

– Tomas Tranströmer

Raven drops into the arms
of the old growth birch.
The trunk's eyes gape, unblinking
at the neat crease of white horizon.

Sleekit winged she perches
Mutters a warning in some tongue
too old for memory.

The fur at the nape of my neck rises.

Weighted by her last feeding—
Muscle memory and bone,
Fur and gore—
Sky pulling her from the tree's axis
A black iridescence praising sky
A velvet unfurling. Lifting.

Wings wide, she wheels off,
a passerine ink-stain
in the milk-pool of sky.
She will return. This is her wood.
Some comprehension that must
never be spoken settles in my gut.

Waxing Gibbous Moon in Cancer

There is something about the experience of trauma. I feel it in me, in my body free-ranging. A constant state of rawness, of how experiencing a loud sound, a strong emotion, a change of plans can send me into overwhelm. And there is the grief. I am noticing the pattern of being forced (a strong word!) to be in the present, intensely present, because both the past and the future seem painful beyond comprehension. The safest and least painful place is in the moment. So curious!

Now that I'm alone here in the cabin, even though I do feel lonely, there is a freedom to just be with whatever the fuck comes up. I cry a lot. Every day I wake up crying and I often go to sleep crying. This feels essential and automatic, it feels like the tidal wave of release I've been longing for.

Four big deaths. Venus, Dad, Mike, and now Bruce. Bruce is dead, (I can barely write about it ... later) in the last 10 months. Too many. Too much. Too soon.

I've been here about six weeks and the rhythms of the sun, the moon, the weather, the woodstove, the chopping of wood (which I love!), and the hauling of water are shaping me into more than just a freaked out, grieving, perimenopausal woman. I am becoming acutely aware of being part of an elemental, sensory world in a way I've never known before. Not like this. I remember feeling something similar when I was traveling and living in Scotland. Maybe because now is the pervasive silent freeze of winter, maybe because I'm still deep in this threshold experience. This relational elemental-ness feels like a blessing. Like a bucket of grace flouncing over, in and through me. Becoming more fluent in the sentient language that I am part of. That is our birthright in this long and short life on Earth. The elements of wood, fire, and water define the parameters of my day.

They and grief are my teachers now.

Another learning curve and teacher knocking on my door is financial stuff. My savings are low. The thought of doing some part- or full-time paid labor feels wrong every way in my body at this time. *Too soon, too soon.* Say my lungs. *Not yet, not yet,* says my heart. *No fucking way,* say my bones!

I've been reflecting on this. Knew the time would come. Other paid work has always kept me from storytelling in libraries during the summer for their summer reading programs. My low-lying fruit is to step more fully into my role of oral storyteller. This has been feeding me in so many ways (minus financially) for 15 years now. Why not start calling libraries and seeing what's possible?

I feel lost and found. I know things I didn't know six months ago, though I do not have language for them. I am hermitting. I am composting.

Penumbra

Though my soul may set in darkness, it will rise in perfect light;
I have loved the stars too fondly to be fearful of the night.

– Sarah Williams, from poem The Old Astronomer in The Twilight Hours

have you ever stood in the middle of a forest miles away from town or home as it gets dark?

Sometimes, in the afternoon, I walk outside into the meadow on the property. This wide-open star gazing space is bordered by second and third growth forest. As the sun slips into the horizon, the snow shines blue. Looking up, as the gloaming comes in, I anticipate the first bright salting of light, old friends. Oh the stars!

There's no light pollution, no full moon. Deep indigo settles in. The forest of birch, maple, and balsam become an amorphous, even darker wall. Night shrouds around us all, and eventually everything becomes indistinct and lost from sight.

Staying put, the cold breaching the layers of wool, my toes, fingers, nose, cheeks begin to ache. My ears hear a twig snap in the woods. I wonder who might be watching. My heart thuds faster. Hairs raise up on my arms. Are there wild eyes watching me breathing, feeling me bristle?

I stay, red-cheeked and waiting. Waiting for something without a name. My nose runs. Fear prickles. I am drowning in the fear of what was, what is and what might be. Memory tells me that the line of birch is just over there, the oak with bronchial branches is there, and I know the cabin's woodstove awaits and yet my heart is exploding with panic.

It's been two months and sixteen days since Mike's death, since our dance.

Now properly cold, teeth chattering, sometimes I stomp my feet, stomp down the fear, bury it in the snow. Sometimes I stay paralyzed, freezing, and rooted in my boots, becoming that avalanche of fear. Sometimes a seductive and known narrative creeps in—if I just sat back into the pillow of snow. So easy.

It's been two months and sixteen days since Mike's death.

It's been one week since learning of my dear friend Bruce's death—heart attack in a Boston hotel room. Bruce was a large human; I guess his heart just got too big and exploded, right across the universe. I can't help consider the logistics of what it took to get his body off the 17th floor. Bruce and his howls of laughter, his ice cream scoop, his Boston Red Socks. Years ago, he told me that anyone who hasn't contemplated taking their own life has yet to plumb the depths of their humanity.

I wonder about that.

These days in the chasm of winter, in this soul-dark night, I feel so fucking lost. I feel the tug of gravity to become earth, in this case, ice. The temptation to cash in all my cards beckons—to surrender to the pain, and the trauma, and the black maw of the unknown.

To just surrender—settle my bones into the snow and there, in the blue hour of twilight, to simply close my eyes, meditate, and let a transcendent slumber become a last exhale. It wouldn't take long. I think of a beloved poet's words and wonder.

Eventually a stronger impulse has me leaning towards life and I'm nudged back to the cabin. Back to firelight, to the teakettle, a good book, to a friend's voice over the phone, to windows and walls, and that tenuous and sensual separation between me and a scalding aortal light.

A Story for the Band

Story is the sweet nectar of language. Story is the crystallizing of thought,
turning it into something digestible, sweet on the heart even when the details
are hard to bear. Story is the way we dribble sweetness over the harsh realities
of life ... rolling what happens on the tongue until we discover the nugget
of meaning, humor, heartbreak and insight.

– Christina Baldwin, from Storycatcher

O*ne evening in early March 2010, during my first winter in the cabin,*
I was feeling restless, feeling cabin feverish. I split some wood, made
a cup of tea, stoked the fire, and sat down at the table with my journal. This
is what poured out. Afterwards I climbed the ladder to the loft and slept for
10 hours. The piece had a life of its own and shortly after I wrote it. a window
of opportunity opened and I sent it to Kevin McMullin, one of the members
of the band, Duck for the Oyster. [vii] *Later that summer this story, along with*
50 other short stories, was published in Roslyn Nelson's beautiful book, Love
Stories of the Bay.[viii]

Duck for the Oyster is playing at Northland College tonight in
Ashland. Part of me wants to go.

Part of me wants to stand in the doorway; listening, watching,
letting what needs to flow and fall. Part of me wants to go sledding
down Manypenny Avenue in Bayfield tonight. To hold on tight and
fly through the night.

If I go to the dance, I'll catch the band on break and say, *Hey, you don't recognize me, but I was the Rainbow dancing in the arms of the Priest at the Halloween Dance last year in Shell Lake. I want to thank you for giving us both one of the best and life-altering nights of our year—of our lives.*

I'll take a deep breath, pausing, looking into their still-listening eyes. The fiddle player will nod at me to go on.

After we left the dance, we drove through the bruise-black night back to Springbrook, sharing childhood ghost stories.

All Hallow's Eve: the night when the veil between the two worlds is thinnest; the night when otherworldliness rules and the night that, according to the Celts, is the beginning of winter and the dark side of the year begins.

Back at Mike's home in the wild woods, we made chamomile tea that sat cooling on the counter while we made sweet love in the arms of the gods and a tattered velour chair.

The fiddle player will lean in, listening. The guitar player will look at their watch. With my eyes lit bright, I'll continue.

Afterwards, we spooned and nuzzled, glowing, purring into each other and sipping the tepid tea (and I suspect he had a swig or two of Pepto on the sly). I told him my transcendental meditation story. He told me I should have won the best costume prize at the dance. I said, "Oh I did win the prize—you." I felt his soft heart swell like a full cat's belly. That night we were falling in love. Humming with it. Love in the food we prepared for each other, the costumes we adorned for each other. Falling in love with each

step danced, eyes softly held. Each caress and each kiss. It was easy to
fall. I was letting go of such weight from my dad's recent death. And Mike
was preparing to let go of the weight of a lifetime.

~

Mike and I met online 19 days before my dad died of lung cancer. He answered my Craigslist post in the platonic section of the personals. I was looking for a pen pal, really and truly, a pen pal who knew the power and mystery of Lake Superior. The lake was a newly found love of mine. I was seeking some normalcy in the wacked-out surrealness that was my life, caregiving for my dying father. I thought having a pen pal would help create some levity, some balance, a bit of desperately needed diversionary fun in these hard-on-the-heart times. A handful of men replied to my post. They all had sweet stories about Lake Superior and I soaked in those with great delight.

My dad, Wayne, was diagnosed in March. I moved in with him in June. By August, I was exhausted. Caregiving for him was one of the most challenging things I'd ever done. He was angry. My dad was dying. In those six months, we both struggled to give language to our impending losses. We ached, watching each other's suffering, and we healed as we navigated this ancient, human, messy end-of-life dance.

Some nights I rubbed his feet and we wept an inland sea of tears.

~

Mike responded to my Craigslist post. We shared the experience of losing a parent to cancer and being the *caregiver* in those liminal times. We shared a great love of that Great Lake. Our connection blossomed into an epistolary friendship which evolved into a listening, laughing, and poetry-reading phone friendship. I shared my story: the hard bits, the challenges. He listened, showering me with such understanding and even then, love. Not a romantic love, but a human, agape-like love.

Mike lived in the dream home he'd built, where, as he confided many times, *Mother Nature's wild glory was just outside the door,* and where *he felt mostly never alone.* Months prior to meeting Mike, I had left my home, friends, work, my life in Iowa to move in with my dying parent in his two-bedroom suburban Milwaukee apartment. There, cigarette smoke filtered up from the downstairs apartment and the tap water carried traces of fecal matter. The nearest friend was a two-hour drive and I felt isolated and drowning in loneliness. To me, Mike was a lighthouse in dark, stormy seas.

After my father passed on, Mike came to visit. It was the first time we'd met face to face. That evening, after riding bikes through town under the canopy of old oak trees, we became lovers. In the course of our days and nights together, we spent 96 hours eye to eye and heart to heart. We played croquet on the back lawn of my father's apartment. We read our fortunes out of cookies with our bellies groaning from hot Thai food. On the phone, from separate homes, we listened to barred owls calling outside our dark autumn windows and we howled with laughter while reading provocative poetry.

I let his tenderness love me, and I gave him the presence seeping from me like sap from a crack where the light gets in. Unknowingly, we were preparing each other for the thresholds ahead. Later, it occurred to me our souls might be completing some pact they had made lifetimes ago on a wild Irish shore—a meaningful fabrication or a deep intuition, who knows? Either way it was a comfort to believe this might be so.

One bright mid-October day I rode upon the saddle of his shoulder taking photos of Mary Nohl's[ix] sculptures—her witchy otherworldly sentinels overlooking Lake Michigan. We sailed kites on Bradford Beach and flew high on the divinity of Warhol at the Calatrava.

Just one week later, on Halloween/Samhain,[x] we danced this perfect waltz like there was no tomorrow. A Rainbow and a Holy Man. We were fluid with the music; feet flowing in step, as if by magic. We were so light, gliding on the polished gym floor. His arm wrapped around my waist. My hand settled into his. His leading. My following. Thighs pressing, eyes shining, grinning like love-struck teens. Unforgettable. It was a dance which redeemed. Never underestimate the power of a man who knows how to waltz you across the room. All around us, in great delight, pirates, queens, wee owls and slant-eyed black cats spun and reeled as the band played on.

The last poem he read to me was Edgar Allan Poe's *The Raven*.

We lived a whole lot of life in those 96 hours.

~

I'd tell the band, two hours and thirty-seven minutes after we left the circle of their music and the magic of that dance, just as we were falling into the cradle of asleep, our toes tucked together, our breath slowing down, Mike's mighty heart stopped. His breath staggered and ceased. Forever more.

~

The fat, shining moon streamed silver across the bed. With my eyes seeing all, his eyes peered far beyond this place. In the dark, my heart rattled like a snare drum—sharp, bright, fast. My hot breath blew into the cooling shell of his unspeakably still body. My blood boomed and gushed in my ears. I pushed and pressed my wide star-shaped hands on his broad sleek chest. In this dance, macabre time slowed down. Way down. Yet my heart was hectic in my throat as I pumped, then pressed my lips to his. And again. I was numb. I was hyper aware of everything. Somewhere in this surreal, shocking tableau, I actually felt his spirit ascend through me. Rising up. Corny and cliché as fuck, but I couldn't make this up.

We had entered into a new dimension together, yet separately.

~

I might not tell the band the mythic redemption that was part of our tale. How after Mike's passing I learned that 20 years prior he was a lost, angry, alcoholic (not unlike my dad). How he'd turned his life around, changing everything—getting sober, living LIFE, rebuilding bridges and re-becoming human.

I learned that his heart was broken when we met and that our brief autumn dance helped knit and purl his heart into something whole.

I would tell the band that—at Mike's Celebration of Life ceremony, his Anishinaabe friend, Little Bird, named him Minnewasa-aninni, meaning Happy Man, in Ojibwemowin.[xi]

I would finish telling my story and we would sit, breathing together, all our eyes a bit wet. Honored to be with these brilliant musicians who played that last dance. I would thank them for their tears, their time, and I would request a waltz. Maybe Greg Brown's *Iowa Waltz* and then ...

Part of me would stay and sway and listen. Part of me would ask the nearest, sweet-faced man to dance. Part of me would turn, walk out to Highway 13, down to the Big Lake and step gracefully, gratefully, in:

one, two, three
one, two, three ...
one, two, three.

Into the wet. Into the cold, cold water. Dancing down. Deep to the ink-black bottom.

Waning Crescent Moon in Capricorn

These last few months, I have spent a lot of time looking down, grounding to earth, anchoring to something solid. Noticing. It seemed to be a practice of being present with myself and all the pain. Looking to earth helps me digest. I also look down for heart-rocks, little *hellos* from him. I'm still finding gifts from him, from the Mystery. These rocks of heart are a bit of delight and wonder—a reminder that everything is interconnected. I am reminded of a potent string of words shared by a qi gong instructor once upon a time in Eugene, Oregon; *I am in the Universe. The Universe is in me. The Universe and I are One.*

Late in February, I went to Mike's house for the first time since that November morning. There was still snow on the ground and the sap was rising and running in the trees. Spring was almost here! As I walked around his homestead and into his home I was soaked by waves of remembering. So many little things I had forgotten in the crush of events.

How that afternoon, on Halloween, before the dance, Mike had to run over to his friends' house to pick up his costume. He also stopped at a local farm to pick up some fresh milk. Another love we shared, fresh, raw milk. When he arrived home, as he was gathering up the costume, the glass jug of milk slipped, fell and broke on the ground. The milk spilled out and was left to clean up later.

Out in the barn, he was so excited to show me his motorcycle with two helmets. We'd planned to take a motorcycle ride up to the lake—a journey we never made, though a much bigger journey was embarked upon. I remembered how he'd given me a tour of his house and all the outbuildings. In the pole barn, he gave me a lovely birch cutting board that he had made. It had that beautiful luminous quality that birch has. That cutting board sits on the counter, here with me in the cabin. It gives me such comfort to use, knowing his hands helped create this.

Mike's woodshed was still heaving with split wood. He loved to chop wood, oh my, and he had chopped enough to last for three or four seasons at least. There was the fire pit he had dug with the iron tripod towering over it, ready at a moment's notice to hold a black iron pot. In the grove of trees just outside his kitchen window, the bird feeder hung. It was empty, unvisited and untended. Did the chickadees miss the consistent stream of birdfeed he offered each winter, all winter, except for last year? How he loved to feed the birds.

Tied to a branch of birch just outside the house was the red ribbon. I had forgotten the red ribbon that I had tied into my hair that night. How the morning after his death, I'd returned to Mike's with my uncle and tied the ribbon in the birch as a marker, as a remembrance.

Returning to Mike's place was something I needed to do. Revisit, to remember. It was part of my healing. With the key in hand, fetched from the hiding place in the woods, I opened the door.

It was cold inside. No fires had lit his space in a while. It was a bittersweet re-entry. Most things were as they had been, though some were not. I sat in the velour chair remembering. I climbed up the stairs and laid down on the bed. It was incredibly tender. I heard an owl call out, unusual for daytime.

Owl reminded me of the phone calls Mike and I shared from Dad's apartment as we were getting to know each other, in our penpal phase. Although Dad's place had been deep in the heart of suburbia, it was surrounded by beautiful mature maple and oak trees where a parliament of barred owls lived. Often, as Mike and I talked on the phone, laughing about who knows what, the owls of Thiensville called back and forth to each other. Some nights, the owls living in the forest around Mike's home would be calling at the same time. Again, the strange and the beautiful.

There had been too many little synchronicities all along this journey. They'd become part of the landscape. So many moments where I felt his quiet and loving presence with me.

I stayed up there for a while longer, looking out the window, Checking out his CD collection. Holding his rocks. Letting the tears fall. Staring at the bed. Next to the bed on the table there was a copy of Michael Perry's book, *Truck*, from the Hayward Library.

I had read it while living with my dad, it was another sweet balm during that painful time. Mike also liked Perry's work and I'd suggested he read *Truck*. He must have borrowed it from the library and been reading it at the time of his death. There was probably a whopper of a fine by now. I wanted to keep it. I should have returned it. I did neither. I hadn't noticed it at his bedside that night. Again, the common and the sublime.

As I was leaving, I paused and looked in the fridge—it was unplugged and empty. I opened the freezer door too. I'm not really sure why I did this. The freezer was empty except for a long slip of paper in the back. How the hell had that gotten there? I turned it over and read.

The soul would have no rainbow had the eyes no tears.

–John Vance Cheney

It was one of the rainbow quotes I had created and gave out at the Halloween dance. One of his kids must have put it there, right? I tucked it into my purse, welcoming it as another gift, a little hello from him, my Miquel.

I am alive.

Sustenance

In the field snow
shrouds last year's husks.
Eagle sits. Waiting.

Sacred through my lens
a soaring god ground to Earth,
I sing myself awake.

Eagle poised to pounce
Awaiting sustenance.
Food for their hatchlings.

Ki's eyes meet mine.
At 40 yards I am a vague threat,
Useless too as my flesh
will not sustain. Or would it?

Eyes linked, ki lifts off
Six foot wingspan casting
Long shadows becoming flight.
Watching I am fed.

Body of Water

Sublime ~ 1. to cause to pass directly from the solid to the vapor state and condense back to solid form. 2. to elevate or exalt especially in dignity or honor. 3. to render finer. 4: to convert into something of higher worth.

I n early April 2010, I drove north in the pre-dawn beneath boughs of oak, spruce and pine. April is always a mixed bag in the north woods and the land was just waking, kissed by both frost and thaw. As I traveled further north, slipping out of Wisconsin along the Big Lake and into Minnesota, the light of the day came gushing in through a bottomless blue sky.

The Irish philosopher and poet John O'Donohue's words swam in my blood that day: *When we approach things with reverence, great things decide to approach us.*[xii] The past too many months, too many losses weighed heavy in me and yet I was aware of how the forces of love and grief and PTS were rearranging my life in uncomfortable, powerful, and beautiful ways. John's quote was a mantra to the swing of my days that winter. That year.

This was a day to honor the hawk poised to feast, and to revere the soft, velvet nubs of the willow. It was a day to honor two lives, two passages—Mike and his infant grandson, Wind. It was also a day to render the leaden load of my grief into something fine spun, something golden. Today was another piece of closure.

Further north, I crossed the Crystal River, pulling to the verge behind a small parade of cars. In concert, car doors opened and a brood of children and their parents spilled out. We gathered in the matted, spent grass greeting one another as the wind sucked each "hello" and "how are you?" upward into the infinite bowl of sky.

This small cove was Mike's favorite place on the North Shore and today we would cast his ashes into the breadth and depth of these hallowed waters. Mike's daughter, Erin would also scatter the ashes of her baby boy, who passed on seven years before.

Booted yet buoyant, we processed up a slope thick with last year's growth of grass. In the vibrant April sunshine, the parched dead blades rustled as we passed, sounding of the sea. I couldn't help thinking this grass, last summer's grass, had grown lush, while Mike had lived and breathed, danced and loved. My hand reached down, connecting with the colorless leaves. I broke off a piece and I brought it to my lips, tasting him.

At the top, we arrived at a clearing, cocooned in the shade of cedars. There at the cliff's edge we clustered, our eyes squinting down to the luminous too-bright water. Someone tied a colorful Guatemalan scarf to a translucent birch and it flapped into the east. Mike's four-year-old grandson had the chosen honor of smudging our rite with sage. His face was solemn, and his blond dreadlocks coiled out from a blaze orange hat as he proudly circled us. The smoke curled around shafts of sun slanting through the cedar boughs, calling in ancestors, bringing the numinous to the forefront. Making this holy.

Mike's daughter, Erin and son Ruairi, stood near the cliff's edge backlit by the sun. The rest of us stood back at a distance holding tight to the warm bodies of squirming children. Erin stepped up to the lip of land. Her baby's ashes spilled from a cloth satchel at her chest. They caught in the wind, suspended. Our breath synced with the swaying trees. We watched gravity draw the pale ash down and out of sight. Her eyes, so like her father's, closed; her body swayed like a silver birch.

Even though I barely knew Erin (we had met once before—at her father's funeral), I felt an abiding love for her. As if that newly minted love for her dad easily transferred unconditionally to her.

Ruairi, Mike's son, stepped up to the edge of rock and buried his hands into a deer hide pouch. His fists drew out handfuls of ash. His palms opened like stars and the wind surged, scattering fragments in all directions. Dusty-ash remains blew into my eyes, powdering my lips. Licking, I drew the fine, dry grains into my moist mouth, tasting. It was sacrament. Handful after handful arced beyond the edge of light and vanished. For a timeless time, we all watched, the scent of cedar and blue filling our lungs.

The eyes of the forest watched too, as we all stood in silence, a collective weaving of experience, and yet each of us singular in our grief. And then I heard it. A sound threading through the branches clear and bright. Someone was whistling. It was a lively tune. I looked left and right seeking the source. I saw no one whistling. The crescent of pebbled beach below was empty. No one seemed to notice the song as it waltzed through the tangle of birch. The tune lifted me. And then, as suddenly as it had begun, it stopped.

What was that? No answer arrived and my attention went back to the ceremony. A fine dusting of pewter, his shining bones covered us all—like icing sugar. The wind had stopped its righteous rant and one by one, each child was led to the ledge to look beyond. The rest of us followed. At the lit rim, gazing into the waves, I saw Mike's ashes; gray and plentiful. Suspended and billowing clouds in the clear water. And there riding on top of his ashes, held by what was left of his body, the wisps of baby WInd's whiter ash. Breathless we watched the two bodies swirl in the wet, in the great body of this mother lake, then disappear into her vast belly.

The brilliance of sunlight on the water, blurred by my salt tears, was blinding —yet I saw everything. I felt my feet plumb down into the sandy soil. Felt the gritty ash on my face, the smell of pine and sage, and all the colors bleed into one.

Something beyond senses, something beyond words, a great widening of perception spread through, conjoining me with everything. Water, air, sun, leaves, sky, stone, flesh, love, creator, and a being known as me, were interwoven and intimately connected.

Eventually, we all pulled back from the edge. Altered, we made our way, goat-like down the rocky, shifting slope to the shore. Erin went off by herself. The children exploded into the fierce play of throwing rocks and chasing the wind.

I sat on the shingled shore in an exquisite in-betweenness. A divine mess, in a great mesh. Eyes looking out to the line of blue greeting blue on the horizon. A heart rock found its way between my fingers. The body that was Mike's is now part of that water. He is of the lake. There was a strong desire to strip down out of my clothes, this skin covering this body, my body, like the way Mike's death had stripped both him and me down, and go into the bright water dancing —but the wind pulled that and all other thoughts from my head. My body folded down onto the sun-warmed rocks.

Later, some of us gathered around a small fire in the shingle along the shore. The sacred feast of this day continued as coffee was made and bread and hummus shared. We spoke of seeds and soil. Of beginnings.

I remembered the whistled tune and asked if anyone had heard it. They all shook their heads except for Mike's friend, Elena, who said she had heard whistling, but hadn't known where it was coming from. "It was kinda strange," she said.

This question mark hung in the air until our collective attention was drawn to the horizon and new-found peace waiting there.

Only hours after arriving, we gathered back on the verge of the highway. The wind carried our laughter and our good-byes out to the shining water. Feeling a vibrancy I hadn't felt in a long while, I journeyed into to the still bright day, back to Wisconsin and Four Mile Creek cabin, my home. Light winked off the lake and the trees bowed along with me in cahoots and co-creation. Greg Brown's voice, low and slow, poured from the car speakers soaking me, tipping me into love with everything again.

Back at the cabin, with a blaze in the wood stove, I set out to get water from the well. Into the gloaming, I walked through the meadow carrying two, five-gallon containers. No snow meant no handy blue toboggan to make the work easier. No matter, a fine night was in the making. It felt good being in my body. Near the well, I stopped, set down the containers and sunk myself into the cold damp grass. I widened my arms and legs, letting everything relax—jaw, back, bum, belly, yoni, shins, and toes. Overhead, the open sky darkened. Stars glinted, salting the sky. Maybe tomorrow I would hike Meyer's Beach Trail.

The Polestar beckoned, *stay.* I was cold. The woodstove beckoned. *come.* I waited. I heard the night sounds in the woods around the meadow. I waited. Soon the sky was both dark and bright. My gaze softened. My whole body hummed. Then each star, an infinity of them, revealed their ancient light, their shining song.

Twenty-four hours from when we'd all stood at the Great Lake's edge, with many miles between us, I finally spoke with Erin. I called to check in with her, and eventually asked if she'd heard the whistling up on the cliff while they had scattered Mike's ashes.

She hadn't heard any whistling. Though, through the phone I felt her smiling. I heard her saying how her dad loved to whistle and was really, *really* good at it.

There was a pause, a long pause as we both sat digesting this. Then a slow blush of goosebumps bloomed on us and in between us. I heard her inhale. And in a simple, matter of fact way, yet brimming alive with awe, she stated simply what we both knew.

It was him.

Initiation in the Green Chapel

Knowing that a stone is alive keeps me alive. And knowing that a stone is alive differently than me keeps me asking questions, keeps me humble, and curious, and open to surprise. This is the Animate Everything.[xiii]
– Sophie Strand from The Flowering Wand: Rewilding the Sacred Masculine

November 2009, Cornucopia Wisconsin

The crushed limestone trail opens into sunlight falling like ribbons through the trees onto November's decay. Once golden, now frostbitten, popple leaves lie grounded—discarded, black hearts. For three days now, this trail has pulled me to the rim of my inland sea, day and day again. This communion of subjects: stone, soil, root, leaf, rhizome, and the 10,000 other-than-human entities have witnessed this movement through the forest's naked thickness. And I have witnessed them. In a mere three days there's a deep kinship with this place, this trail. Each day I become more intimate with this forest, the trail and their multiplicities. I wonder, I imagine how they might sense this broken, wide-open human who has come day after day offering the only things I possess: raging grief, raw sentience and love. What might the trail see and say if only I could hear? A boreal chickadee defies the crush of decay, bulleting joy through the birch. I know the way.

We feel her, boots treading firmly over us. We are wet and leaf-strewn. An ancestry of rock and clay, intention and sweat, and a maze of mycelial thread. We are the network of paths curving and intersecting along this stretch of forest, of earth, of place. Winding through the family of white birch, cedar, silver birch and white pine. We are more than this trail, hugging the shore of the Great Lake, staying close from a distance. We are the middle ground between bush-whacking and aimlessness. We are a way. Down. In. Up. And out of the woods. Here at earth level, we see more than you would imagine.

Today I less feel heavy. The cleansing has begun, thanks to the land, Lake Superior, and time. Twenty-one days since Samhain, since Mike took his last breath. The grief-pain coloring my blood courses thick and viscous and yet there is a narrow flume of grace inside me now. My boots hit the earth, the underbelly of my soles meeting the crushed lunar gravel of the trail, keeping rhythm. My breath comes deeper, and there are so many unanswered questions.

We have not always been so distinct, so easily marked. Before two-leggeds traversed upon us, there were hooves, and paws, and the footless slither of bellies impressing themselves, defining us as a path. Then, two-leggeds arrived speaking the language of forests, of lakes, of Earth and Sun. They revered this place, they saw us all, honored all life. Now many of the two-leggeds who come have forgotten. They live in an oblivion of us. And yet some feet do listen, do see, feel, know, and remember the birthright of our conjoined connection. On this brisk morning of decay, we are glad of her feet, again. For the past few days, she has been the only one to come.

All six senses are awake. It is trauma, or grief? Both! Have I lost my mind? More questions. In this altered state I feel the rise and fall of this land, the reaching tall cathedral birch of ki, the bear paws and fox claws who journeyed along this trail. I hear the fritter of chickadees zipping from tree to tree, the seiche of the Lake just out of sight. I see the broken bones of windblown birch scattered, rotting. Tasting salt tears dried on my lips, seeing my footprints from the days before, knowing my story is now woven with the story of this place. This is both meaningful and meaningless.

My feet fall square and heavy, slow and thick, but my mind spins and flashes like a top. Three weeks ago, my lover and I danced a masked All Hallow's Eve waltz. Unmasked, we made love, and we nestled into that love afterwards. Cooing into each other, our feet tangled, we easily fell. Into sleep. Into love.

Now his feet are ash, and I am the tied-too-tight knot remaining.

We feel her heaviness, her otherness. We feel the strong light within her simmer, shimmering. The weight of her presses into us, smoothing our sharp stones. Her story of loss and grace bleed through her into us. We feel him. Here with her, loving her, wanting to help. Asking questions.

That night, our last, just as I was drifting into the limbic space before sleep—we were two warm hearts quietly beating in one bed, two mouths breathing, ebbing, flowing with the sprouting promise of us—from just under the lintel of sleep I was pulled back to waking by something, a presence, an absence. And then, my heartbeat pounding, alone.

Now along this trail, along the Big Momma Lake, my body moves through the trees with its shattered heart, and this whirly-gig mind on the trail we had planned to hike—one day. For three days I've come, pushing slush earth, dancing my grief, stomping, wailing, rejoicing and planting salt tears as seeds. Yesterday and the day before I beseeched Source and Mike to fill me with grace, praying for just one outrageous grief-induced miracle—that in our love making that night we would have conceived a child.

But today I bleed – the third day on the trail, my blood flows out. Delusion. Illusion. Dissolution. I step one foot, after the other, roaming, seeking ceremony from birch to birch.

We call on the cedar, the long, wet branches to surround her, doubly cloaking her, wrapping her in the leafy hubris of life yet powerfully tasting death's ancient story. She walks—lamenting, celebrating, singing to the forest. With the vacant hunger of an initiate, from silver birch to white birch she roves like a winter butterfly pollinating the trees with her pain, with her acceptance, and with her grief.

And we watch as she, in this holy green chapel, reaches down past the waistband of her skirt dipping into her core, drawing her finger out—slick and crimson with her blood.

And we watch as she steps up to the blank canvas of a white birch and presses a small perfect ruby-blood heart onto ki. She leans into the tree, whispering, incanting, glowing, and gifting.

April 2010

Five months and thirty-six inches of white Superior snow since I last walked this trail. I'm here again, feeling the rising renewal of my deep-rooted winter. Yesterday on Minnesota's North Shore, we released Mike's ashes. His clan gathered, bearing witness to his next journey when air, water, sunlight, all merged into one, and the earth-loving dust of his physical form scattered from the hands of his children into the fluid mystery, into Gichi-gami.

The snow has gone. The swollen rush of creek water intersecting the trail has ebbed. The trail is clear.

We are thawing, numb and mute.

Today is to integrate yesterday. To flow and feel the woods gather around me, to feel the gravel, clay, loam, and red sandstone bedrock endlessly solid beneath my feet. Bowing low, I honor this budding of life, the soft song of a tufted titmouse, the murmur of ravens. Honoring these life-filled woods. This greater lake. Humbling to the space between the layers of grace and grief. To the enormously minute growth from there to here. It is spring. *Birth* is the word gushing all around. I am becoming. Suddenly alive. Suddenly potent. Suddenly transformed, stepping further along the trail.

We feel her footfalls and rouse from our winter's slumber. We see and recognize her—barely. The weight of grief that she wore like a tight shroud then, now drapes loose, flowing behind her. There is fire in her eyes as she steps through the melty-iced pools of mud. Her eyes are wide and we watch her step along the just-emerging ribbon of us.

Listening into this cusp of land at the edge of a sea, I drift under popple boughs fat with spring's promise. Assimilation. Sublimation. Regeneration. The trail rises budding and sunlit. A familiar path, the same, yet so vastly different. Like me. I remember back to my last visit, the wailing and beseeching, and the precious offering I'd left behind—the small blood heart. How had it fared over the winter? Could I find the tree?

We remember her heavy-footed death march, her animal howls of grief as her blood flowed. We remember as she marked her place, her love in the world.

The day is bright and I pour myself into it, seeking. New life is birthing from every mossy phyllid and every budding cell, soothing the still-sharp shards inside me. All this new life distracts me from my search. I let go of seeking. Does it matter that last November's blood stained a tree? Did I need to see it to believe it? No. The trail's hoarse voice rang, *You are the heart, and the blood, and the bark, and the blue, and he is the lake, and the air that seeps and gushes into your hungry lungs.* In that moment, just as the day before on the clifftop, all the colors, subjects, and identities bleed into one. There is no separation; the trail and the lake and the birch, his spirit, my blood, my cracked and beautiful heart, are unbound and together.

We are wide awake now, her life-force linked with ours. She is new leaves, clear water, fresh, wet earth and spring wind. We watch her move up and over, with and along the boundary of us. We are the trail, into the woods, along the Big Water. We have always been. We are traveled by hoof and foot and paw. We have been the path for the hunted and those who hunt, for those who stroll, and climb, and gambol, and run. We watch and we wait. We see her cross the stream, becoming the stream, climb the rock steps, becoming the rock, gaze at the Lake, becoming the Lake.

Over the wet red earth, over last autumn's leaves and the wet of winter's snow, breathing, my feet moving, feeling lighter. I am of the trail now; down the slope, over the creek, up the steps. No seeking, no questions or answers. Moving deeper into the woods.

Halfway up a rise on the trail, breathing deep in my lungs, pausing, eyes lighting on one tree, a birch. One of a hundred, one of a thousand. *Come*, this birch tree whispers. Magnetically drawn, climbing higher, further up the hill.

We watch as her attention falls on a tree. She approaches this slim, tall silver-white birch. Love spills from her eyes as she leans into ki, as she wraps herself around ki. Her forehead gently presses into the silver bark and she breathes in. Her softly humming lips purse, press, and kiss.

My two hands reach, feeling the slim cool trunk, belly, cheek, forehead press into this silver birch swaying. Arms folding around this beckoning, stretching-to-the-sky birch. We are breathing each other in and out. In these breaths, unexpectedly a flood of love and desire surges.

Touched, bewildered, then softening, becoming even more still, gently settling my lips and pressing them into the smooth electric bark.

Time slows way down.

Coming to under the dome of sky and crosshatch of branches; content, dazed, embarrassed. The waking sounds of the forest meets my ears. Pulling away, yet still connected. Thankful, wondering, curious, lingering, laughing, alive, breathing in and out, I step back, and begin walking away. Betwixt and between, bemused and befuddled. Looking back, I take one parting look at this tree lover. This magnificent birch. My gaze falls onto the back side of the tree, the side that's been hidden to me. And there it is. Faded but clearly marked. A gray heart-shaped stain. Waiting to be seen.

July 2010

They meander together, yet separately through the dark boreal summer-tide forest. Sun spills through the lush canopy lighting his lake blue eyes, her red lipped smile. We are the trail and we see. We feel. So many, they come to us, to the forest's mystery, to the land's song, to the Lake's love. We see her, with a man, a man whose feet have never traveled us. A man more human than spirit. A tall, reaching, birch of a man. It was her, the one who had marched and danced, yowled and offered a stream of hot tears upon us. She who had marked the tree, bright with blood. She who had come back again, whisper-ing, pressing herself, her love into that silver luminous bark.

Shyly, firmly they hold hands as they walk upon us, their new love, their soles/souls pressing into us, into each other, weaving through the birch, blessed in the cool shadows of this majestic chapel green.

Waning Crescent in Virgo

I t's been one year today: twelve months, thirteen moons and about 8.5 million breaths. It has been a haul, an epic, an unimaginable, wild ride. It has been a quest. Never again will I be the person who pulled up to Mike's house last Halloween, rainbow costume in the backseat, weary, curious and opening to his love. So much to grieve. To hold. To digest. To let go of. I still don't know if I'll get out of this chapter alive and yet there are times when I have never felt more alive. Ever.

I now chop wood, carry water, and feel the life in me as the same life in the tall, reaching red pine, in the white waves of my inland sea. I feel mighty and broken. Expanded and contracted. I am the fecund goo, neither caterpillar nor butterfly. Becoming something else. Other.

A year ago, Mike and me were tipping and tumbling into it. Was it love, fate, karma? Maybe all three. I've been rereading the trail of emails between Mike and me in the weeks leading up to his death.

There is something about revisiting, remembering these correspondences. There is something about remembering what it was like to be in the middle of a very stressful place, living with a dying and angry parent, feeling so weary, sad, isolated, and alone and *yet* also feeling grace spilling in slantwise. Liminal experiences shifting my shape. I didn't know what grace was until Dad's illness and Venus' death.

Oh, my Venus. I can barely think of your bright eyes and curly tail without some part of me receding, hiding, still, a year and a half later. It's the part of the story I rarely mention. It is still hard to think of it, of you. When one loses the love of their life and that love is a black cat so sleek and elegant, so loving, so in tune, some folks don't get that part of the story. But her death on D Street, two weeks after Dad was diagnosed, broke open the grace door. I was driving the freeways of Milwaukee's east side, heading to pick up Dad from his chemo appointment. U2 was blasting through the speakers, spring air poured through the windows, and howls of pain spilled out my mouth. And then, something opened. I felt an immense peace, like honey flowing through me. It didn't stay for long, but the memory of it sustained me for the feats of endurance ahead.

Grace arrived. I had a handful of ashes in one hand and a handful of gold in the other. Grace was like a drug that has ebbed and flowed through me, coloring my perception over this past year. Grace, my own between-worlds place while my beloveds around me journey on to theirs.

After Mike's death. Just as we were falling asleep. Falling in love. Then, like a kite taken by the wind. Zooop. Gone. Not in the body. Breathless. Still. Dead. Yet, grace trickled and sometimes gushed in.

Then Bruce—dear fairy godfatherly friend. Like Mike, big ass heart attack and he became, just like his favorite Beatle's song, *Across the Universe*. That's what I felt. That's grace.

Now Patrick, alive and well! This dear, golden-hearted man who has stitched his way into my life, my story. He's a tall peak of grace. Strange to accept this intuition which has come back again and again, that *Patrick is a gift from Mike*, and in some inexplicable way his place in my life was born out of loving and losing Mike. This feels like truth in my body.

And this grace is still with me, seeping and soaking, buoying me through the pain. It's been over a year since Mike's death and there is so much rawness, such preciousness layered in with the day-to-day of life now. I have come to learn that each precious breath is a poem, then, if we're lucky, it's followed by another. Each chance to dance with the wild other-than-human-world, a cherished gift. I am still swimming in the ashes and the gold. Tucking in for another winter in the cabin ... after that, who knows?

Reading *The Layers*, a poem by Stanley Kunitz, has been part of my daily practice. This poem feeds me and one line in particular, "Live in the layers, not on the litter." seems a mantra for me at this time.

I am full and empty.

Waxing Gibbous Moon in Pisces

Summer Solstice, Dad's birthday. He would have been 72 today. I miss him. Miss talking about new music, single malt, and hiking. Miss our hikes along Lake Michigan at the Schlitz Audubon Center and chocolate custard at Gilles afterwards. Sad to say this, I appreciate him more now. Is that common?

I am leaving this little slice of healing heaven here along Four Mile Creek. 'Tis time to gather all the bits of this cabin life—the axe, teacups, quilts, books, rocks, and all the stories. This place, in the cabin, in the woods, near the creek and not far from the Big Momma Lake has been sanctuary. I feel a bit teary about it and yet it's the next step. Endings and beginnings.

I'm moving to Menomonie, Wisconsin, near another lake, Lake Menomin, to be with Patrick. After a year of a long-distance relationship, it's time. I'll sublet a flat and then if things go well, I'll move into his house maybe in August. We are taking things slow. It feels good.

More to come!

I am okay. I feel curious, open and sad. I am blooming.

What Fell from the Moon Last Night

The peace behind everything
is the unstory beneath us all,
is the emptiness we forget
and remember.

The unknown on the horizon
is the place we seek + hide from,
is the endless sky-well of mystery
we drink from.

The bright chord of wonder within
is where all is born and dies,
is the fertile dark + white feral thread,
is the peace, and the mystery,
and the only way in and out.

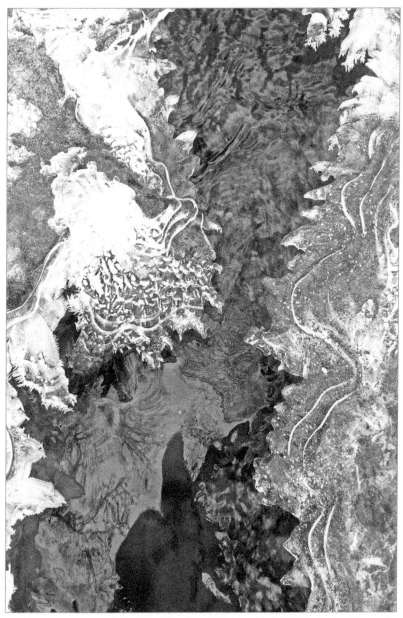

Lake Menomin, Wisconsin

Lake Menomin

more-than-humans:

robin, Canada geese, rabbit, maidenhair fern, columbines, chickens, lilacs and a black cat called Pippin

playlist:

Bon Iver, Kate Tempest, Ma Muse, Converge Radio, Tom Morton's Beatcroft Radio, Low the band, *Do You Realize* by The Flaming Lips, a distance train, peals of laughter and wailing tears of neighborhood littles

libations:

RO water, Pu'er Tea, Nonic Brewery British Bitter, fresh-made almond milk

nibbles:

eggs from Trixie, Hazel, Sweet Pea, Mabel, Tilda and Honey Bun, kale, green beans, rose petals, Tom Ka Ga soup, almond cakes

stories:

East of the Sun West of the Moon, *Corrag* by Susan Fletcher, endless insomnia and laughing 'til breathless in the middle of the night with Patrick, Hazel the hen, and Preparation H

Waxing Crescent in Virgo

I am here. I have left the Big Momma Lake (for now) for love.

Patrick and I are living in the same town and that has been sweet. Very sweet. I have over 15 summer storytelling performances lined up in libraries and even a few house concerts!

And now my story unfolds here in Menomonie, near Lake Menomin. Not Lake Superior, though still a body of water with a story I'm getting to know. It's been three weeks. It has been quite a transition from the cabin, from chopping wood and carrying water to an apartment with plumbing! I'm finding it a rough transition in many ways, except for with Patrick. With us. Our curious and growing relationship is the best part.

Making friends in a new community in your late 40s, without kids or a traditional workplace feels tricky for me.

I am making friends with longing again (whom I know well from all those years weaving in and out of Scotland). I am missing the north woods, that wild life, those wild woods, and wild silence that was part of the warp and weft of my days and nights. I know that silence is still in me, yet I am finding it harder to feel it, connect with it in the hubbub of a neighborhood in a city.

Before I left the cabin in June, I was taking baths in the meadow with the singing, greening forest, the soft bright sun, and late spring breeze all around. And while having plumbing and hot baths is pretty damn good, I am remembering those moments of aliveness—feeling the sun, and the wind, and freshly-pumped and heated well water on my body.

With this missing comes the longing ... dear old friend. So I am stretching myself between these two places along Lake Menomin and north to Lake Superior.

I will go back. The Lake is only a three-hour drive north and north! I have storytellings coming up there, so soon.

I feel grateful. I have a garden. I feel less broken. I love and feel loved.

Beheld

A lake is the landscape's most beautiful and expressive feature.
It is earth's eye; looking into which the beholder measures
the depth of his own nature.

– Henry David Thoreau

early summer and the sky is a bottomless blue and the watered waves mirror light and infinity. Just days past summer solstice, and the canoe carries my beloved partner Patrick and me through Lake Menomin. From our doorstep, the lake is a 10-minute walk. For the past year and a half this landscape of western Wisconsin is home. The lake is both a great comfort and a sharp fishbone in my heart. She carries hidden stories, old wounds, as do I.

Lake Menomin is a small lake. At first glance, she offers a scenic expanse above and mysterious depths below. There is no doubt that Lake Menomin brings light and wonder to this community, though her present and past is complex.

Menomin means *wild rice* to the Indigenous land ancestors of this place; the Ho Chunk and Oceti Sakowin peoples who tended and inhabited this area. Menomin is food. It is life. In my cabin near the Big Momma Lake, wild rice harvested from small lakes nearby nourished me over those two winters.

Lake Menomin begins and ends on the Red Cedar River. The river flows 100 miles from its source in Northern Wisconsin until it weds itself with the Mississippi. This lake, named for the sustaining staple, is a dammed-up reservoir created during the logging boom by prominent European-American men—lumber barons and the founding fathers of Menomonie. Like the ancient trees of Northern Wisconsin, this lake holds the ghosts of ancient peoples; the Ho Chunk people whose burial grounds along the river were desecrated when the river was dammed up to create the lake.

Knowing this will not change one of thousands of transgressions, these sharp fishbones of colonial wounding, but it might break your heart, tenderize that precious muscle and make you feel. Wake you up.

No permission was granted. No reparations have been made, to date, that I'm aware of.

This human-crafted eye of Earth stretches out to now re-forested shores. She is a mixed bag of light and shadow, like us all, like me. Here in this still-new to me, more southernly, yet still northern home, I dance between drinking in the promise of new beginnings and the heavy weight of the old stories I carry.

The lake is at her best in spring's first blush, before the heat of summer turns her clear water to sour green algae bloom. And here, in this place, some days, I feel a sense of my former, more innocent self until something triggers the PTS, and the frequency of anxiety overshadows that budding re-growth and the still smoldering bonfires of rage reignite.

At midsummer, the lake begins to foam and froth. Her man-made shadowlands surface as the chemical fertilizers from upstream agriculture fill and choke. I find myself unable to swallow and digest the breadth and depth of all that has happened in these past few years. If I could just split some wood!

By August, a marbled layer of green sits slick and thick on Lake Menomin's surface. Is she expressing our imbalance, mirroring our societal disregard for the Earth, showing us our own polluted depths? Inside me, my depths too feel tainted. Even with the 'comforts' of plumbing and the ease of walking through the neighborhood to the shops I feel myself going under, struggling to stay afloat. I feel suffocated by the proximity of neighbors, of traffic, of people, by the trauma both conscious and unconscious still living in my body. I need the peace of tall, reaching trees, the grace of long-shining big water. I need the wild silence of north.

And, I do wonder, is there a place deep and centered in this seemingly corrupted man-made lake? Does such a place live in us? In me? Could there be a river of origin where all flows clear and free, where that wild silence always lives? I am searching, I am praying, for evidence of this in her, in us and in me.

There have been attempts to clean up Lake Menomin. There are dialogs with farmers upstream. The best theory I've heard involves draining her, letting vegetation reclaim her, nature clear her. Let her become wild and unsightly. I've been told it wouldn't be good for economic development. I know it would be good for me.

From afar, even in the full heat of summer, Lake Menomin shines like a wet gem. Come closer to her foaming edges, and the loss is visible and felt. Come closer still, please don't look away. Notice her acid-green waves. Can you relate?

Can you witness the putrefying parts in you? Feel those festering parts, the deep losses in us? I notice the acid waves of trauma, anxiety, and rage in my own water body. Can you?

And sometimes, when my listening is robust, I feel a beckoning of what might be—what could be possible in her, in us. I must look deeper, down into our most silent stirrings, and there I can sense a pulse of life, a quickening of power, a glimpse of new life inside her/us/me.

Perhaps it is there, deep in her fluid heart, where she, and we, are gazing out, lens both clear and murky, beholding and reflecting, us and All.

Becoming *Of*

To be of is to hunker down as a servant to the ruminations of the specific
valley, little gritty vegetable patch, or swampy acre of abandoned field
that has laid its breath on the back of your neck.[xiv]
– Martin Shaw, from Small Gods

I n my youth, the language of Wisconsin's nature sang singsong in
my ears from my childhood home of Wauwatosa, meaning *firefly*
in Potawatomie: Lake Michigan's ever present and unlanguaged
scent, morning glory's blue-blazing bloom, and the rough and
familiar comfort of elm leaves in my palm, were all within reach.
I was always listening. Always sensing. Always feeling. These, plus
a thousand other breath-by-breath gifts, offered themselves up to
my fledgling sentience and I welcomed them in as, I sensed, they
welcomed me. We opened to a portal of mutual high regard.

Over time and geography, the many worlds of Wisconsin and
beyond claimed me as family: the wildwoods of Gad, my childhood
always-near knowing of Lake Michigan, and the ancient geography
of the miraculous Driftless Region, which has never known the ebb
of flow of Ice Age glaciers. These all served as guardians of my youth.
Then, into adulthood, the unexpected homeplace of Scotland, the
deep intelligence of Oregon's old growth, and the unspeakable
vastness of Lake Superior, all became familial allies. Even the strange
jewel of Lake Menomin is part of my family tree of places that have
claimed me as kin. These relationships held me, the way family

might, allowing the expression "becoming of" to become a felt sense. And over the years, at times I have forgotten the blessing of this *of-ness*. I have moved, as we often do, into an oblivion, an amnesia. Now, in the middle of my life, autumn stretches out, and I am picking up the threads of remembering. Here once again, in the land of my birth and the birthplace of my blood relations, I am remembering what I have forgotten about being *of* place.

Each day, from the small front yard of our Menomonie home, hundreds of honey-colored leaves release and fall, magnificent and profound. A golden blur eddying in the wind, playing chase like children of the sun until their masses wither to crackling detritus. Looking up, the bones of maple reach for all six directions. Their naked limbs raised in praise, vulnerable once again to the north wind, to night shine. I remember. I listen. I sense. I feel. I raise my arms in praise and humble myself to an essential part of this ecosystem, a small part of this luscious wholeness!

Down below the litter of leaves, the earth lies moist, diggable. Further down lie the bones and dust of my European pioneer ancestors. The worker bees of religious fervor, colonization and industrialization, of places now known as England, Scotland, Norway and Germany. Thick-skinned farmers, homemakers, birthers of babies and babies and babies, women of secret, unfulfilled dreams. From Loyal to Milwaukee, Gad to Cadot, my lineage is planted here within the borders of this place called Wisconsin. The name-sounds of those who stand behind me: Ros-a-lyn, Le-ona, Wil-lis, Lo-rin,

Laur-a, Ar-thur, Mag-da-lena, Will-i-am, Way-ne, and now Lor-na. And all those standing behind them who crossed the Atlantic with armloads of Old World wounds and promises of betterment. In the end, we are all sutures of poetry, the terrible and beautiful, quilting and embellishing the path behind, this moment now, and what is just out beyond the horizon's edge.

Digging deeper, gathering courage, acknowledging that there at the rim of bedrock, moraine and Ice Age stories, are the spirits of the Indigenous peoples who are of this land in a way I shall never be: the Potawatomi, Ho Chunk, Anishinaabe, Menominee, Oneida, and Oceti Sakowin peoples. Humbly asking to be in relationship with them and with their wounding. May they all rest in peace. May our re-membering be a drop of precious water in the sea of their healing, for all, across all time. May there be reparations. Justice. An epoch of equality.

As the lemon-sun leaves drip, as the veil thins, as the patch of pebbled garden dies back, as the old ones, my beloveds, reduce to rebirth, I step *from* this place, leaning in humbly, listening, declaring my *of-ness* with this land, a land known as *Meskousing, Weskohsaeh*[xv] and as Wisconsin.

To the swale of moraine—holding. To the eyes of water—seeing. To the sanctuary of forest—singing their lullabies without words. To the deep inland sea—shining life. And to our all relations – remembered. Honored. Whole.

A Place I Sometimes Reside

Reside: late 15th century meaning "to settle, to rest, linger, be left.

The winter after my grandparents passing within a month of each other, the first winter their home was no longer there, I noticed a squirrel's nest built precariously in the outer edges of an old, large maple tree bending out over our street. In the late winter, I passed it daily as I traveled to and from work.

Maple, reaching gownless, limbs —wildly gesturing.
This habitat of wet wood stretching, rising, thawing.
Sap tunneling through heartwood, becoming black bones.

Woven into the sinew of this tree being, a den.
A dreamcatcher for those nesting at home, inside.

A collection of brown, sturdy leaves, a musky space built of necessity. Each leaf carried jaw by jaw in morning's scampering light. Each leaf and matted tuft of fur tucked in and out and through the limbed mesh.

A place of feasting and birthing and nut-glutted slumbering, sewn fast by industriousness and the ceaseless winter wind. Remarkably still a safe place in the wild churning boughs of the tree. Still anchored well to the great hum beneath.

Great Spirit, will you wed me to this? This perception. This simplicity. This illusion of safety. A den of my own sedulous crafting?

Will you cloak me in tawny fur, weave me into the tangle of leaf and twig, feral for one day? Warless, politic-free, and utterly unconcerned with blethering fools. A respite from my grief.

Will you leave me here to be open-eyed, settled, safe to gaze up and up, through the crosshatched maze of this den and the sap fed limbs, into the hull of blue-black eternity?

Into the star shine, singing sea shanties to the moon?

The Listening of Winter

... only when one comes to listen, only when one is aware and still,

can things be seen and heard.

– Sigurd F. Olson, *Listening Point*

The Earth is days past perihelion. The sun, at its low-slung zenith, perches white and untouchable. Temperatures range between minus 22 and 4 above zero, Fahrenheit. There is a rare luster to the light that at 16 degrees would be some other, lesser light. I love these biting cold days.

Some days I head to the horizon of thick ice on Lake Menomin, seeking antidotal balance from the four walls, the screen and street traffic. I seek the tongue of black ice, the hoard of snowy glamour, and the quiet prize of water flowing just a few feet beneath.

This is the first winter without them, Leona and Lorin, and without a place to rest and be in Gad. Feeling rootless and often lost. Some days, weeks, are anvil heavy, and sometimes I'm possessed by an expansive joy that I know is part of grief, for joy is kin to loss.

Today my heart is full and light; I'll take it. On route to the lake, I stepped into a grove of pine and a maze of tracks: fox and squirrel, deer and human, an interspecies layering of paws on the refreshed canvas of snow. Signs of their activity, mostly under the cover of night, makes me happy—happy that they have chosen here as their home. My tracks add to the map of to-ings and fro-ings. My prints, like squirrel's, trek from tree to tree. Like fox, my tracks start, stop, back up and shift directions, revealing movement with a meal in mind, though my meal is this moment. I step with attempted deer grace through the banded shadows of vertical pine on snow.

At the indistinct snow-clad edge where land meets the shore, I step off frozen earth onto ice. There's an immediate internal *ahhh,* and a subtle compass inside my body tells me I am not on solid ground. Without seeing the obvious delineation marking where land meets water, thanks to the snow, this nuanced knowing is a beautiful soul tending practice. This is my superpower. I'm grateful for the knowing that this shifting of shape, from land to ice, from the Big Lake to this smaller lake, and from life to death/death to life, is the music of what is.

A stiff, subzero wind greets me, and with eyes squinting, cheeks reddening, I bow my head and walk onto the two-foot-thick ice. More silence, fewer city sounds allow a deeper level of listening; I hear the black velvet flap of crow's flight, the tectonic groaning of ice, and the clock tower bell baffled by cold and distance. Not far, up the steep rise of a hundred stairs, houses sit. Further on, the hum of the nonstop interstate drones. Straight up, the gibbous moon shines like an egg in blue space. I feel light here on the open-wide white. My body crackles, joyous with a sense of aliveness and freedom. My mind empties. My heart thunders and icy in-breaths slowly warm. Exhaling, I step forward.

Yule Dreamtime

I.

A visitation in the hush of night.
The old lights – stars and moon
through the gauze of cloud.
The haze of too bright streetlights,
are enough to see your shadowed tracks,
reveal padded ponds of blue on the dark white.
Coyote, you trickster. You muse.

II.

Coiled snug in her downy nest,
pink wine gum nose snuffling
in and out, in and out rabbit rhythm
in her snow-buried burrow.

The cranberry blush of her veiny ears
tuned to moist unfrozen earth close beneath.
Dreaming her places of clover and sunshine
of rapid, quick-quick matings,
of broods of pink wiggling babes
of milk white—spilling onto fur.

Full Moon in Virgo

I t's official, I am over the threshold of "official" menopause. It has been 12 cycles since my moon. At the Equinox, I'll do ceremony to honor this major transition. It feels momentous, and there is grief. Unexpectedly. Grief for the absence of a sacred cycle, a monthly shedding, for the absence of blood, which, as annoying and as messy as it was, was a sacred, holy time: to rest, release, and honor self-tending time. Grief for what it might mean to be barren, like those beloved Scottish Western Isles, often described as barren, yet so utterly, blessedly fertile with so much language and life!

Patrick and I have begun looking for a small parcel of land for sale in Washburn. This is absolutely a long shot dream. Mother Superior still calls. The dream: a wild place of boreal forest. A place to steward. A place to find sanctuary. T'would be a miracle.

We've visited one parcel a few times, last autumn and over the winter. It's still for sale. We are watching and waiting. Eeeeeeeeeek!

We are both carrying small, shining, carnelian red agates from Meyer's Beach with us as talismans to what's possible. He thinks it's a bit weird, and yet he's doing it. So, we are resting in this possibility! Eyes, toes, and noses crossed.

I have over 10 libraries booked for summer storytellings so far and thanks to the inspiring work of wise humans: Clarrisa Pinkola Estes, Sharon Blackie, Michael Meade, and Martin Shaw, I am sinking deep, deep into myth, ecology, and fairy tales, as transforming allies essential for our evolution!

I've been engaging with storytelling and children since 1995, and in the last five years, I have deepened into more storytellings and courses with adults. To my next edge! So very rich. What I'm noticing is that while children love engaging with stories in this ancient oral way, they are naturals at using their beautiful imaginations, and for the most part can easily sit for an hour-long storytelling with ease. Adults are such a different experience. My experience thus far is that adults struggle to settle, to put down their devices (and I am guilty of this too!), to listen and imagine actively. Yet when they do, and they can stay awake, there is a deep hunger, a need for these stories. Playing the sole role of entertaining folks isn't for me. I want to dive into the story together; fully present, alive, and ready to be transformed. That's when some magic happens. That's alchemy! That's where the metamorphic gifts of story live, and where I want to play.

I see changes. I feel charged. I know what is, is all there is.

A Crone is Born

I am a Queen leaning into Crone.

Raven sits on my left shoulder

12 moons and no release. No shedding. A bloodless womb.

Another significant death to digest.

I am biologically infertile.

Two unborn fetuses, released (mostly) by choice stand behind me,

More precious now, for the spark they were,

for who they could have become.

And, for the privilege of choice.

Culturally, I'm told I'm becoming invisible, until I will be.

Barred from the Life-Giving-Initiation

Great-grandmother Magdalena lived through 15 times.

Grieving for this unspoken, under acknowledged rite of passage,

Making peace with lost pieces of motherhood.

What will now birth from the crucible, the womb of my life,

Visible and more whole than all the decades before?

Waxing Gibbous in Aquarius

Feeling the lightness and the weight of many anniversaries today on All Saints Day, in the threshold of Samhain. According to the Celts, the winter season and a new year has begun. The harvest is in and now is a time for rest.

Feeling grateful for this season of composting and moving toward the frozen silence of winter.

Ten years ago today, I learned Transcendental Meditation in Eugene. It was a day of sweetness, innocence, and anticipation, feeling so grateful for this daily practice which saved my ass, literally. I honestly do not know if I would have survived the past five years without it. Feeling so much gratitude for Bruce, the man who instigated it all. Bless, bless, bless, him. I miss him ... holy shit, do I.

Five years ago today, ahhh, Mike Scoles took his last breath, body still tingling from our waltz and our lovemaking, and five years ago today, my life as I knew it, changed forevermore. I both miss the woman I was before this epic event, and can't really conceive who I might be without it.

And then the still tender, tender loss of Grandma and Grandpa, just over a year ago. It was a year ago that their house was sold. It feels like I lost Gad too. It's like three mighty losses in one. Jeez, this one still hurts.

I know so little, and have both lost and gained so much. Life is paradox.

New Moon in Libra

T is a time of the best news and (what feels like) the worst news! Last month we made an offer on a small parcel of land just outside Washburn. The owners were in a hurry to sell, so the price was dropping and dropping. The offer was accepted! That which seemed impossible is really happening. The land is raven's land, and fox's too. This land is Anishinaabe land, and as stewards, we will not forget that. There is a seasonal stream that meanders through this place, so we call this space of 10,000 life forms Meanderland. Next month, we will put in a driveway and then someday a small dwelling. Seems like a dream! So grateful and still in shock.

The news that really, really sucks is this—I have Lyme disease and,though feeling better today, shit, it has been a rough few weeks. The antibiotics are finally helping, though I dread thinking what they are doing to my gut.

All summer, I've been doing part-time work gardening and enjoyed such blessed hours in the prairie-scape of an Eau Claire home. I pulled and pruned, tended and communed, with friends: Partridge Pea, Beebalm, three types of Milkweed, Liatris, Aster, and magnificent Joe Pye Weed. Each night I checked for ticks. Then at the end of the season, after days clearing tall-reaching Joe Pye

Weed, also den of grasshoppers and spiders, I found a little red bite on my right shoulder. That little red bite began to ulcerate, and the tell-tale double bullseye of Lyme disease bloomed.

And more good news (I think). In a week, I'm meant to go on a three-week trip to Scotland. Oh, back to that sweet soul home. This is something my friend Pam and I have been dreaming of for years. She retired and we began to make this happen. She's never been there, and it has been 11 years since I've been back, walking that majestic land!

The plan is still to go, Lyme or not. We'll meet in Glasgow. We'll have a few days in Edinburgh, and I'll take her to all my favorite haunts! Yippeee! I am so excited, I can't see straight!

From Edinburgh, north we shall go to Ullapool along Loch Broom, then Achiltibuie, a place I've not been before. Then we'll take the ferry over to the Outer Hebrides, to Lewis, and then to the ancient ones—Callanish. At some point after that, we'll take a bus through Harris and the ferry to Uist: *Tir a Mhurain*, the land of bent grass.

It seems like a dream sometimes, that I spent years in Scotland, from 1992 to 2004, back and forth, arriving and departing in all seasons, living, walking the land, ears full of the islands' music! All those years, listening and soaking in the depths of the *machair*, moor, shore, and mountains and language and people of that place. Still feels like a dream!

In all those years, only one friend from stateside life came to visit me in the Isles, so I am freakin' over the moon to be able to share these precious islands with Pamela Ann. Fuck Lyme!

Once again holding the ashes and gold.

I see old patterns holding me and new opportunities ahead. I feel excited and exhausted.

Helplessness and Appetite

There was an embrace in death.

– Virginia Woolf, Mrs. Dalloway

Under a blank canvas sky becoming twilight, we walked to Lake Menomin. My fifth winter in courtship with this place. Out on the thin newborn ice, a Canada goose struggles to free an iced-in leg. We watch.

Every few minutes, the goose presses dark wings into the translucent crust. The only thing of color, one bright orange webbed foot, pushes against the cold surface. Ki's elegant neck lengthens, straining for release. Seeking liberation.

Then ki rests. This cycle of straining and rest continues. We stand witness to this dilemma. Powerless from the shore, a half hour passes. Our breath rises to halo the waning moon, and we make for home.

We knock on the neighbor's door, waking him from a lazy Sunday nap, "Is there someone we can contact? Can anything be done?" He says, "That goose is cooked unless the ice breaks up," giving a wry, sleepy smile.

The next morning, I walk down to the lake's edge with binoculars, hopeful in the light spit of mizzle that I won't need them. Hopeful that the wind broke up the ice and ki has flown free. Just imagining that goose in flight, somehow frees me a bit from my own helplessness, just for a moment. Lyme and the endless months of antibiotics are eating me alive.

I hear the crows first, as I come to the edge of the partial frozen lake. Then, I spot the eagle. Through the binoculars, the only things of color are the sun-yellow beak of eagle and the rust-red lump of goose. Heavy in the heart, yet transfixed, I watch eagle pull strands of this meat from between their talons.

From the shore, frozen to the core, a half hour passes.

Impatient crows wait. Once fulfilled, eagle lifts shroud-black wings wide, and with a power and grace that defies me (that Lyme has denied me), ki rises into the gray and away.

The Thaw

Sloping in slant-wise under
Trickster crow's wing,
Robins sing arriving
Songs from the upper
Tangle of maples. The sun, an
Unblemished peach eases
Gingerly to the lip of land.
Lingering, just. A. Moment. More.
Over-ripe snow gleams liquid
Yet still frozen.
Once powdered pristine,
Now dimpled and pocked by the
Skitter of those pin oak leaves
Who held on through every blizzard,
Who only now in this blushing spring
Give themselves to the wind,
Scraping over the curdled milk of old snow,
Their mad maze of tracks leading to a melt hole
Where crocus flares forth,
And fat maple buds listen to the din of children's
belly-laughter on swings.

Can I too give myself to the thaw?

Sated

Full UP

Teeming with microbes

Brimming with late May showers,

They, our Kin drink and drink.

Rain splashes, rushes, trickles

Rivulets blessing all.

Spider in her neat filigree corner quenches.

Beetle bordering on a hallucination lolls, succulent

Yarrow stalk reaches, singing.

Tall grasses drunk on downpours,

Gulls soaring clean and bright,

Precipitation churns the clouds, shrouds the sun

Wild wet reigns again!

So be full and fat,

Revel in this just-birthed spring harvest

It is all we have and soon enough the pebbles shall

roll dry in the dust remembering the perfume of petrichor.

Waning Gibbous Moon in Capricorn

happy 77th Birthday, Dad! In honor of your birthday and summer solstice I will eat some blended frozen banana, which is as close to frozen custard as I can get!

Ahhhh! Last summer was the *last summer* I would roam relatively carefree through the woods, off the trails and paths. For years now, I have taken precautions to prevent tick bites and yet ... they found me.

I am 10 months into my journey with Lyme disease and I am weary. Seven of those months I've been on at least three types of antibiotics. Between the Lyme and antibiotics, I am completely gutted. My microbiome is demolished. It feels like I am allergic to everything: all grains, legumes, dairy, starchy vegetables, and most fragrances. At the hint of any of these triggers, my body plummets into an autoimmune response of aches and hives, headaches, bloating, and fatigue I have never known before. I suspect, somewhere in the mix of this illness, borne of trauma, lives all the other bits of still partially-digested traumas: early childhood sexual abuse, familial emotional abuse, teenage pregnancy, and too many deaths too soon, too close together.

The past seven years since Dad's diagnosis have been an unprecedented descent into both deep, deep shadowlands and the golden solace of the most silent places inside me. Thank all the names of God for my meditation practice. For the grace that does still claim me, with robin's evensong, with lilac's riotous perfume and with my breath breathing me.

I feel restless and a waxing and waning at peace-ness.

Communion of Subjects[xvi]

Honoring the losses of Alberta's Fort McMurray wildfire.[xvii]

10,000 spirits wrapped in summer clouds,
ushered by the northwest wind
Came softly after such brutal raging.
After the thousand-mile journey dusted in stars.

Drifting in through the night-washed window.
An incense of lost and found,
A three a.m. waking while
the world around slept.

For days this veil of ghosts draped over maples,
wrapped round lampposts occluding even the sun.
The mighty remains of jack pine, spruce.
Tracts of needle and thread grass, beaks and bones, all ash.
Burnt offerings in my lungs – both foreign and known
Consumed, consummate, a sorrow, a loss.

The sublimation of a living world,
now falling ash—effortless as snow over the taiga,
dispersed by wide white wings of Saskatoon swans,
digested by frog spawn dining in Lake Manitoba and
compost for the lady slipper's threaded roots.

Who says there isn't enchantment in ashes.

Where is the story behind God?

Lost and Found

People like us, who believe in physics, know that the distinction
between past, present and future is only
a stubbornly persistent illusion.

– Albert Einstein

e are moving—from the bright yet tarnished, gaze of Lake Menomin to the Gichi-gami. After 11 years residing here in Menomonie, just a jog from one small lake, at the northern edge of the providential Driftless Region, I am returning—we are—going north, to the Big Lake—to Meanderland.

This means the basement is a morass of stacks and piles waiting to be sifted and sorted. The treasured detritus of all my relations. Oy!

Deep in the mix of my father's cameras, my mother's card making supplies, my grandfather's flannel shirts and piles of Grandma-made quilts, I find a basket shaped like a sand pail, and I am flooded with remembering. This basket was my grandma's. This is where she kept her stash of hair rollers for as long as I could remember. The rollers had bristling inner skeletons and outer wire mesh. There were all sizes. Some were light blue, some a grayish black with pink and white plastic pins. Grandma was an expert at using them. She knew how to lance the pin through the heart of the roller at just the right angle, wedging it tight to her wise pate. The basket sat in her bathroom cupboard with jars of Dippity-Do, Pond's Cold Cream and tins of Watson's carbolic salve. Her holy trinity.

~

We lost Grandma in early August. One month later, Grandpa made the journey.

In the loss born of their departure I inherited a curious and mundane medley of their possessions: Grandma's Chicago Cutlery paring knife which had sliced 72 years of apples; her basket of hair rollers; her hope chest, still fragrant of cedar; their 1950s vintage *Homer Laughlin Autumn Gold* dishes; and Grandpa's compass. All treasure.

~

With the passing of years, I had forgotten about the basket in the basement. It was empty now. The rollers gone. At the bottom, three rusted bobby pins sat. Seeing these made me smile, they had easily been down there 40 or 50 years. I rinsed out the basket and wiped out the ancient fuzz and bits of accumulated detritus. As I dried off my hands, I noticed a flash of white on my right forefinger. There, perched like something spun from a fairy tale, was a silver white hair. Neither too short or long. Lightning-bright and curled. It could only be Grandma's. Leaning in, listening. This finding from the basket whispered stories of too tight perms, bright wind-flutter-ing scarves, Aqua Net, and the buttery goodness of fried potatoes.

A silver gleaning from her. A thread in the weaving of her story, as I stood by the sink letting the swells of ache and joy lap over me.

Ode to a Tick

You ugly, crawling, spindle legged devil
Dark pinprick of mayhem.
Lurking quester of feral forests,
Thwarter of peaceful communion,
Leveler of creed, gender and beast.
One sucking nip from you, all bacterial hell breaks loose—
A lifeforce altered.

Inciter of caution,
Deep caller of awareness and
Demander of robust immune systems worldwide.

You have offered me a gift.
Strange spiraling spirochetes
Embedding inside
Every tissue with a message.

Slow down.
Pay Attention.
Tend to the garden of my body.
For six years I have prayed at your altar
Stayed to the well-worn path
Spring, summer and autumn
Forgoer of bushwhacking
Made humble by you and 7 gut wrenching

months of antibiotics.
I bow, still daily
To your mighty miniscule greatness.

I shall take my wild roaming
To the winter woods cloaked in the subzero,
Dazzled and bewitched by the singular brights
Of blue-white shimmer. Free of threat
Reclaiming life.

Blessed by Winter.
At home in the snow.

– a nod to Robert Burns' To A Louse, *with deepest thanks
to Mrs. Laport for the introduction*

North

Twelve years ago in the bitter-cold heart of winter,
   North called me.
From Gad I drove north on Highway 13, my car brimming
   with home-making things;
books, rocks, Grandma-made quilts and my dad's axe.

North with my broken-open heart.
Listening to Peter Gabriel's album, "Us."

North to a primitive cabin on Church Corner Road, near Four Mile
Creek, not far from Gichi-gami. It was -14 F and snow was so clean
it was blue.

There a wood stove and no plumbing. I chopped wood and carried
water, literally and spiritually.

For two winters my north-dwelling heart healed some and my
whole being courted fire and ice, life and death, grief and grace.

~

Now, in the bright blessings of spring I travel north from
   an old home in Menomonie.

North again on Highway 13, my car filled with home-making
supplies: books, a laptop, sheets and a little gold fox I found in a
local shop.

North to a new home, my heart a diamond (a bit chipped and dinged up). Listening to Tom Morton's Beatcroft Social, live from Shetland.

North to a primitive cabin on Peacy Road, near a meandering seasonal creek, a mile from the Mother Superior. The ice is melting, fat buds opening.

There is no electricity, no plumbing, and a wood stove. We shall chop wood and carry water, literally and spiritually.

This is Ojibwe land. Both Patrick and I are aware of the privileges we have, that allow us the honor to steward this small parcel of Earth, home to birch and raven, fire and ice, life and death, grief and grace.

May we open to our aliveness, live in the questions, in concert with wild and bodacious life.

North.

Nether Largie Stone Circle, Kilmartin Glen, Scotland

Scotland

more-than-humans:

swan, gorse, bog asphodel, crotal, peat, magpie, Lewisian Gneiss, bracken fern, rowan

playlist:

Half Man Half Biscuit, The Waterboys—*Fisherman's Blues*, Iain MacDonald, Paul Brady —*The Island*, Radio nan Gàidheal, the gale-force wind, the swell of riotous laughter erupting from the mouths of cailleachs on Hector's bus from Daliburgh, Iain McLachlan's pipe tune—*The Dark Island*

libations:

tea, 80 Shilling, Fraoch ale, uisge beatha—Laphroig, Bunnahab-hain, Bowmore, Bells and Talisker, Iron Bru

nibbles:

herring fried in oats, chips with brown sauce, neeps, Wine Gums, Mary Johnson's scones, struan with Cathie Walker

stories:

Donnie MacRury telling *The Beasties Causeway* on Clachan Moor, the monkey at the afterhours party in the pink house on Portree quay, and Seumas McLeod's Loch Skipport stories

Spirit Speaks

I no longer pray—
now I drink dark chocolate
and let the moon sing to me.

I no longer pray—
I let my ancestors dance
through my hips
at the slightest provocation.

I no longer pray—
I go to the river
and howl my ancient pain
into the current.

I no longer pray—
I ache, I desire,
I say "yes" to my longing ...

– Chelan Harkin, from Susceptible to Light [xviii]

The wet, autumn-faded landscape of the English midlands streamed by through the National Express bus window. The bus seats were covered in a vibrantly outdated. geometric pattern and smelled of onions. We were seven hours into this ten-hour journey, heading north from London to Edinburgh. It was October 1992, and I was still pinching myself that this was happening.

I was in Great Britain, an ancestral homeland. A place I had inexplicably longed for and dreamed of since I was young. Over the past four months, I had quit my teaching job, bought a one-way ticket to London, and sold most of my worldly possessions. Now I was heading north to Scotland. I had a 30-day roundtrip bus ticket, a place to stay near Edinburgh, and a plan to see where spirit led me. To the Highlands? West to the Isles? I had no idea at that point. After 30 days I planned to return to London and then travel to Spain.

A kind and chatty woman sat next to me on the bus. She shared her twiglets with me, and in her mellifluous voice, told me about her rose garden. I listened, while stringing beads from a tray in my lap.

The landscape began to shift the further north we traveled. The broad, open swell of the Midlands morphed into the hills and dales of Yorkshire. Next, we crossed into Northumberland National Park. The bus rose and fell with the sweeping moorland. The landscape unhinged dramatically, revealing a large-as-life expanse; the tawny gold-green of autumn bracken and fading heather met the cloud-clotted sky. The bus seemed to teeter on the penknife of the world, and I felt that at any moment it might topple right over. Awe doesn't come close to expressing what met every cell of my body/being.

One minute it was just me, gobsmacked by the majesty pouring in—eyes round with wonder. Then the length of my skin erupted in goosebumps. Tears streamed down my face. Inside a voice (my voice?) rang like a bell in my head, *I'm home.*

Lightning bolt.

I'm home. I had no meaning to connect with these words or the vast feeling sweeping though my body. I had no prior association with this place. Home had always been Wisconsin—Gad, Milwaukee, and La Crosse. They were the only three places I'd ever known as a home place.

That one experience shifted the course of my heart, my spirit, and my life. I would not use my return ticket. I would stay in Scotland longer: walking her holy land, dreaming her shorelines, listening. That day, a lifelong courtship had begun.

Waxing Crescent Moon in Capricorn

T is the threshold of Samhain, the time when the veil between the worlds is thinnest. Samhain, or the modern day Halloween in Scotland is not as commercialized here as it is in the States—no surprise there. Last night, I spied a few kids carrying around pillowcases to collect treats, as they go door to door. This is part of their custom as *guisers.* Their disguises were simple and homemade. I'm glad I was able to see how they celebrate.

So far, my time in Scotland has been completely eye opening, jaw dropping, new, and yet strangely familiar. Edinburgh is the most beautiful city I've ever seen.

I've been in Scotland for over a month. I did not use my return bus ticket last week, back to London, and I have no plans to leave any time soon. I'm staying with an older couple in Dalkeith, which is just outside Edinburgh. Their son, Iain, was heading to visit friends in the west, and I was ready to start exploring beyond Edinburgh, so he agreed to take me as far as Oban.

Last night, as we drove north and west from Edinburgh, we passed through Glencoe. Even though it was very dark out, I could sense the land rising up from the floor of the glen as we drove through, holding the ribbon of road and us, speeding through the night. Even though I've never been here before, and couldn't see a bloody thing out the window, I had a knowing and feeling of the land around me. It gave me goosebumps. I am taking this as a sign I am right where I need to be on this amazing adventure.

Last night, we stayed with Iain's friend outside Oban. When we arrived, there was a peat fire going which smelled and felt amazing after the long drive. I felt like the ignorant American, which I humbly am.

They offered me a glass of whisky, Scotch to us Americans, which I'd had a sip of once a long time ago and didn't like, but *this* whisky, *this* was ambrosia! Buttery and sweet, like liquid gold in my mouth. It was heaven! It was a single malt whisky called Bowmore, from the island of Islay. As we sipped this gorgeous, amber liquid by a sweet peat fire, stories of our journeys spilled out. What an unforgettable evening.

Today I'm taking the ferry from Oban over to the Isle of Mull and then to the holy island of Iona. The light here in the west is transcendental.

I am a harvest.

Waxing Crescent Moon in Cancer

F inally made it over to Islay. I'm in a small, stone built, converted chapel called *St. Kilda* with a whole wall of books. The weather has been deliciously *dreich* (gloomy) the whole weekend, so I've cloistered myself off and read Milan Kundera's *Book of Laughter of Forgetting*. Super powerful! I love his work, celebrating the breadth and depth of life, and death. Traveling and being here in Scotland has taught me that I want to live a life of depth and breadth. I'm not sure what that means exactly, though I think I've felt it here. Moving forward, I will live more rooted in the questions—discerning where/when I experience depth of experience and when I do not.

I called Dad today from a red phone box in the middle of the wild moors of Islay! He was so surprised. It's amazing, I just put in 50 pence and the phone (which reeked of cigarettes) connected me to his place in Milwaukee!

Last week after seven months traveling without my moon, without my holy crimson cycle. I bled! Ahhhhh! That was a homecoming. My biology has finally synced with the rest of me and the stinging irony is, fuck me, I will be heading back to the States soon. Too soon! To celebrate the arrival of my period and soon-to-be departure of these Celtic lands, I bought a flowery red dress!

Tomorrow I'll head back to Edinburgh for another week, then London and then back to the USA. Big swells of feelings around this.

If Scotland is a *she,* she is flowing in my blood. If Scotland is a *he,* he has become my bones. If Scotland is neither she nor he, they are a panoply, a riot of life, language, history, alive through the lens of my experience. I am heartbroken to be going away. What will I do without the wet and the wild to keep me company, and the snell wind, and Auld Reekie, and the music and Craig, Amanda, Barry, and the Dalkeith clan? Arthur's Seat, Tobermory, the fox-gloves and blue bells, Callanish and their cousin circles, and the salty banter? The whisky! Ach, noooo!

I'm afraid something wild and newly awakened inside me by this place will wither and die. And yet how could that ever leave me now? Ever.

It is time for the next chapter of my storybook. Ach, aye! Feeling like a walking contradiction. Sad, sad to leave and curious and just a little excited to see what life awaits me in the states. Curious to see what life has in store for me, what I will create and experience next.

My first stop is Wisconsin; to Gad, and Grandma and Grandpa! This is the longest stretch of my life without visiting them. I'll get to see my dad too. From Gad, the plan is to keep the momentum going and head to Oregon where *my once upon a time love,* is waiting. Dear Jeff. Why not? I suspect this won't be the first or last time I move to a new place for love. I've heard the Pacific Northwest and Scottish landscapes are similar. I will soon find out.

Right now, I am here, on this gorgeous Inner Hebridean island surrounded by the sea and this extraordinary, transcendent light. And many lovely whisky distilleries! *Slainte!*

I feel changed ...

Alba[*]

A thousand shades of gray
colour a thousand shades of stone.
Soon I'll be without you, all alone.
'Tis a shame to feel such sorrow
facing such a bright tomorrow.

But oh, my bonnie lass 'tis hard letting go of the past.

I landed on your misty shores wet behind the ears
with a deep knowing I'd been here for years.
I've danced and played upon your moss
to leave now, could be a loss.

But oh aye, my bonnie land, in my soul there's a Scottish space.

The page is turning, a season's changing.
To be sure, tears I'll be shedding.
A place of green and gray, mist and moor,
Friends and brew, the auld and new.

Oh aye, my bonnie place I'll not be forgetting you.

- Written on the plane back to the States, June 1993
* Alba is the Scottish Gaelic name for Scotland.

A Living Art

*O*nce upon a time, there was an old man and an old woman living
away up in the north and the west of Scotland. Further north than
most folk would consider ever going. They lived at the edge of the sea and
had a small croft. They had a cow, a few sheep, and a handful of chickens
so they were never hungry. Healthy as horses they were. Those beasts were
their pride and joy.

Well now, the day came when the old man, who had lived a very long life,
was ill and on his death bed. It was the custom in those days to keep vigil
with the dying so they wouldn't be alone. Also, it was the common practice
for those on their death bed to speak out their last words; maybe a confes-
sion of some wrong needing to be righted, maybe something they needed
to get off their chest before crossing over, or maybe divulge a secret stash
hidden in the bog. Anyway, that's the way it was and still is for some.

So, the poor man's wife was tending to him, and he kept trying to speak.
He was clearly agitated and very weak. She watched him try and try to say
something, but the words would not come out.

She thought maybe a bit of water to wet his parched lips might help. So, she
stirred her finger in a jar of water and wet his lips. The old man licked his lips
and strained to speak, yet no words came out. Well, his wife thought, maybe
a bit of milk. So, she went out to the byre to get some milk and brought it to
her husband's side. She stirred the milk, warm from the coo (cow), with her
finger, and wet his lips. She watched her husband of 60 some years lick his

lips, then give a faint smile. He tried to speak. He tried and tried but naught, no words. She tutted and soothed him, "There, there, now, now. 'Tis all right." Well, this went on for hours and hours.

Now, being the keen wife she was, she knew where her man kept his bottle of uisge beatha, the water of life: whisky. Now she didn't take the stuff herself, though she knew he liked to have a nip now and again. Ach, why shouldn't he have a bit of comfort here at the end? So she went out to the loose stone in the side of the house, wriggled it out and drew forth a bottle of whisky and brought it back into the bedroom. She poured a good measure into the cup with the milk, the lovely, fresh milk, still warm from the coo. She dipped her finger in, giving the whisky a good stir with the milk ... and she wet his lips.

The old dying man's dry tongue flicked and licked his lips. He licked and licked some more. Out of his mouth he croaked, "More." So she stirred the milk, laced with whisky, and wet his lips. The old man licked his lips and his face lit up like a sunburst on the sea, a smile spread across his weathered old face. He sat up a bit and mouthed the word, "More." So, she stirred her finger in the whisky milk and wet his lips again. The old man licked and smacked his lips together, his eye grew wide as saucers, and if you'd really looked for a moment, his old eye twinkled with a rare light as he tried to speak. He gasped and struggled. He sputtered and spiddled, and then, with great effort, these words tumbled out,

"Don't ... (gasp), don't ... don't sell the coo!"

And then he fell back deid (dead).

That's it! xix

Storyteller David Campbell, eyes blazing with this story, looked very pleased as he finished his wee tale. He read my slightly perplexed face. "Don't sell the coo." he said. "If you had a cow giving whisky milk, that would be worth a fortune! So don't sell the coo!"

~

Edinburgh has been recognized as Scotland's capital since at least the 1400s and a settlement as far back as the early Middle Ages. The rain-slick cobblestones of the High Street are heaving with centuries of stories: stories of war and granite heavy sorrow, stories of black plague, and the insane hysteria of hunting, trying and executing thousands of women branded WITCH; stories of poets, royalty, buskers, students, lovers, barmaids, merchants, drunks, and tens of thousands of merry Festival goers. This ever-flowing river of stories haunts the High Street, from Edinburgh Castle at the top to Holyrood Palace on the bottom. On a rain and shine May day, I moved through these layers, listening, sipping in the salty sweetness of stories old and new.

I was in Edinburgh for a few days before heading north and west to the islands for my first three-month trip with the Hebridean Folklore Project. The Hebridean Folklore Project was a grass roots nonprofit organization with a mission to help keep Scottish Gaelic folklore alive and accessible. It was the dream which I'd been laboring to birth into the world since my visit to the islands in 1995. This beginning was a threshold place in my life and as

I ducked under the lintel, stepping up the winding stone stairway of a High Street café, I felt ripples of excitement and the wild unknown rushing like a river in my body. I'd arranged to meet with Scottish storyteller David Campbell before heading north to the isles.

David, a wise, witty, and distinctive character, and also the reigning king of contemporary traditional storytelling in Scotland, arrived in his kilt. He wore Birkenstock sandals on his wool-socked feet, his silver-gray hair was pulled back in a slightly disheveled ponytail, and his eyes glittered with life.

I told David I was heading to the Outer Hebrides. I told him about the Hebridean Folklore Project, and my desire to help keep the folklore of the islands alive and make it more available to any and all keen to know. David said if I was going to the islands, I needed a story to bring with me, an offering to the land and those good folk. Then, with his eyes shining like the sun, he told the story of *The Dying Crofter and the Coo*. He also said, if I was going into the very heartbeat of Scottish Gaelic culture, I needed to have a musical instrument to play, and sent me on a wild goose chase through the closes and cobbled streets of Edinburgh to find a penny whistle, which I did, to bring along with me.

Over the years and visits to come, the story David generously told me that soft May day was often the gift I offered, along with a packet of chocolates, and sometimes a small bottle of whisky, into the ears of elders from Barra to Harris. This tale told orally was always well received. Laughter reverberated in those thick-walled crofter's kitchens and forged many bridges between place, time, and culture.

Horizon Horse

Storytellers are characters that drink at the creek of eternity,
then communicate such refreshment within the rudiments of time,
so others feel the benefit. Their tongue becomes the runway
between the timeless and the time bound.

– Martin Shaw

T ucked into a worn comfy chair, with a packet of biscuits between us and a magnificently hot strong cup of tea in my hand, I listened, leaning in, breath held, as Mary Ulph told her tale. Images and sensation filled me as I followed the river of her story. She was going back and forth, recollecting in her mind and in her speaking; one minute she was with me, her rheumy eyes peering into mine, then, those cloudy eyes would part and the sunshine of her memory carried us back to when she was wee.

Scottish Gaelic was Mary's first language, her dialect specific to the village of Stoneybridge, on the western and southerly side of the island of South Uist in the Outer Hebrides of Scotland. Mary had lived in Stoneybridge all her eighty years with the heaving North Atlantic literally a stone's throw away. She knew a deep intimacy with this place. Mary, like many of these islanders, knew the language of the brutal wind, the wilding sucking sea, and the transcendent island ight.

Her whole life, Mary knew the lullaby of *murhain* grass singing, and the clamber of shingle tumbling. She knew the scent of summer machair; ^{xx} and the red shank's tune.

On this late summer day, Mary spoke in English as she remembered another day when the weather was fine, as it often seems to be when remembering our youth.

She spoke of a pair of horses belonging to her father. One gray, who was fairly good natured and a hard worker. The other, named Star, was all black with a patch of white on his forehead. Star was a bit of a handful. As the sun poured in through her kitchen window, and the Rayburn gave off the warm tang of peat, she spoke.

This Star was always spooked and very stubborn. I kind of liked him, he was always sweet with me and sometimes I took him a carrot, which he loved. He had the most beautiful eyes of any living creature I'd ever seen. He eventually got the work done, so I guess that's why my father kept him. That, and there wasn't really any money to buy a new horse.

Anyway, I remember a day, well, the sun was shining so bright on the sea it hurt your eyes to look on it. My father had the horses hooked up to do some plowing on this wee strip of land along the shore. The machair there was rich and fertile and was the best place to grow our potatoes. It was a good day, what could go wrong? Well, one of the horses got spooked, the one who was always in trouble, Star, and the way I looked at it, better that he was in trouble than me.

Anyway, those horses took off and that ornery one was leading the way. They were heading right for the sea. The other horse, the gray, had enough sense to release himself and run up the shoreline bucking and running like the devil himself was on his heels. The other, Star, went straight in the sea—plow and all. We called after him, trying to get his attention, hoping he would turn around, but naught. He must have been a strong horse 'cause he just kept on swimming, himself and the plow. That horse was on a mission. I remember feeling exhilarated, maybe that was what the horse was feeling as he swam and swam. I was scared, too, for it was a sure thing that horse would drown and our plow too. That was going to be a hardship.

I thought about the horse. When his energy and determination began to ebb, when the ocean became too strong and the weight of the plow would start to pull him under, what would Star be thinking about? I'd grown up with those animals and even at my young age I knew horses did some powerful thinking. They were much smarter than any cow, sheep, or chicken I'd met. What was that horse thinking as he swam into the west? I wondered if he felt freedom? My father had a fierce look on his face. My little brother began crying and we watched our mad horse until he was just a speck on the horizon, then he was gone. Into the setting sun.

This was all pretty exciting stuff and it wasn't long before the neighbors had heard about it. That night, we had a ceilidh and folk speculated on what happened to that horse. My father told the story quite few times; each time there was a bit more excitement in the telling.

What a story! The next morning, we were all up looking to see if the tide had brought the body in. Nothing. The children of Stonebridge walked for miles *in both directions along the shore, but there was no horse, no plow. For a week or more we watched for Star. After a while we stopped wondering about the horse, but we never forgot. My father got a used plow and managed to get enough money together to buy another horse. Folk still talked about the horse. It was kind of like the story of the summer, it was kind of like a joke. We almost felt famous for being connected to an animal like that.*

What a horse! Well eventually some other story or happening became the new talk around Stoneybridge. Anyway, about two months later, we heard that someone had seen our horse up in North Uist. Angus John was visiting his sister in Baleshare and he said he was sure he saw a horse that looked like the one that swam off. Well, I guess that meant we had to go pay a visit to Baleshare. So, one Sunday after church, we found a lift to North Uist. That's a story in itself to tell because back then there were no causeways between South Uist and Benbecula, between Benbecula and North Uist, or between North Uist and Baleshare. I guess that's a good place to finish the tale for now, having you wonder how we got to Baleshare and what we found when we got there.

Sin a gade! [xxi]

The curtain closed over time and memory for Mary. She started, then gathered herself up as if she'd lost herself for a moment. I think we both had. With worn gnarled hands and a smile dancing on her lips, she poured more hot tea into the teacup glued in my hand and held up the biscuits, saying, "Here have some more biscuits, it's a windy day out there, can't have you blowing away."

That story filled the four walls of Mary's kitchen. That story sat in our laps and I swear I heard a horse whinny on the other side of the back door.

Mary's story, the deep generosity of her presence, the warmth of the Rayburn stove and the gloaming's stunning light spilling in, filled me up in ways I had forgotten.

I felt a familiar tug of longing for Gad and my grandma as I gazed through the window out to the west and the wild Atlantic.

Later, I tumbled out of the warmth and geraniums of her kitchen into the long shadows of the afternoon. I had about three miles to walk to catch the bus or catch a lift back to Benbecula. The murhain grass was a shimmering sea of waves animated by the biting wind. The ceaseless Atlantic was rolling upon the shingle, and feeling humbled, I began the walk home, filled with story, utterly gifted.

Fragment^{xxii}

Mar a bha,

Mar a tha,

Mar a bhitheas

Gu brath,

A Thrithinn

Nan Gras!

Ri traghadh,

'S ri lionadh

Nan gras!

Ri traghadh

'S ri lionadh.

As it was

As it is,

As it shall be

Evermore,

O Thou Triune

Of Grace!

With the ebb,

With the flow,

O Thou Triune

Of grace!

With the ebb,

With the flow.

Once Upon a Place

... The centuries emerge and the lapwing calls:
Pee-wit! Pee-wit!
I sight it through the gathering dark,
Push at the water with my idiot hands
And steer my clumsy craft towards it.
– Tom Hirons, from Lapwing Stars, in Falconer's Joy[xxiii]

There is a place scattered and sculpted by wet and wind and deep, deep-time ice. Islands dropped into the mercurial waters of the North Atlantic: an archipelago—the Outer Hebrides— where the once-inhabited cliffs of Mingulay to the south stretch to the storm-dark Butt of Lewis in the north. These Western Isles, as they are also known, are home to *tir a'mhurain,* the land of bent grass. There the layers between ancient time, the present-day and the living land weave and intersect with the strata of linguistic and cultural influences of the Pictish, Celtic and the Norse Peoples.

On these islands, I came to know the layers of language and stories living through the landscapes and the generations of those woven into this place. I came to know something ancient and alive, inexplicable, and utterly distinct from places I'd known on the mainland. Over the years, there would be many arrivals and departures to and from these Western Isles and with each visit, a marrow deep immersion into the Indigenous oral language—

Scottish Gaelic, the machair, the stories, the sea, the songs, and the salt-scoured moors of these islands.

On my first journey to the Islands in May 1995, I was soaked with an elemental connection with the places I'd met near Bornish and Stoneybridge on the island of South Uist. I thrived with the wild wind whipping, the salt spray blessing, the ancient stones humming in my hands, and the sound of Gaelic ebbing and flowing in my ears. Inside me something shifted; both a breaking open and a soothing. The word ringing in my head wasn't *home* though, something like *here and now*. From that first life-altering encounter with the Western Isles, a mutual regard was born, and from there, a series of events gave birth to a very grassroots undertaking called the Hebridean Folklore Project.[xxiv]

The story of that birthing is this: how one night, translucent blue twilight pouring over the lochs of North Uist, my ornithologist friend Craig and I got into a deep conversation with a local gentleman about the status of oral tradition and folklore of the islands, from the snug of a local pub. We listened and learned about local oral traditions and that, while there were still stories known, folks weren't sharing them much anymore. Memories were fading, life moved too fast, and at that time, young folks weren't really interested. We learned that the status quo of the time was that many of the stories and songs collected over many decades, often by academics and journalists, tended to be inaccessible to the average person on the islands or beyond. After hearing this, something stirred in me. I felt there was perhaps another way possible. From that conversation, and my experiences visiting with folks on the islands at that time, I was inspired to take some kind of action, and that action eventually led to founding The Hebridean Folklore Project.

Through the Hebridean Folklore Project, I had the humble and honored experience of returning to the Outer Hebrides, year after year, deepening relationships with the land, her, and with their language and stories. Any attempts to convey the grace of these encounters, like trying to describe the numinous, falls short, and yet I can't help myself: crossing the causeway in the pelting rain, from North Uist to Grimsay to visit Mary MacLean, a lauded bardess; walking the heathered Clachan Moor with Donnie MacRury of Stilligarry, a deep encyclopedia of folkloric knowledge; laughing with young Helen Walker as we made our way over the single track roads on foot from Daliburgh to visit local poet Donald MacDonald of South Lochboisdale, who well into his eighties still thatched his own roof; the many, many visits with Cathie Walker of Daliburgh; peals and peals of laughter pouring into the dreich night, trekking the isolated stretch to Loch Carnon to drink hot, strong tea with Mary MacRury, the local genealogist; and wandering the saddle of Ben Corodale with Seumas MacLeod, stories of his childhood in Loch Skipport ringing clear as a bell over the bracken.

My memory banks are full to brimming with these holy moments, like that one *garabh* (wild) November afternoon, as a gale frothed the sea white. Near the end of my five-month visit, I found myself seated near a peat fire with Norman MacLeod of Leverburgh, on the Isle of Harris. Norman was brimming with stories. Stories from his childhood and from his many years as a police officer on the mainland. One story was about a particular landform, *Caolas Sgàire*, out in the Minch off the east coast of Harris. As a boy, his father took him out fishing there and told him this story about the Cailleach Sgàire.[xxv]

The Cailleach Sgàire lived in Lochland (now Norway) and for whatever reason she was exiled from her homeland by the king and sent south. The Cailleach eventually arrived on the island of Eire (Ireland). She grieved and longed for her homeland, though she took solace in this new fertile land. The Cailleach grew a beautiful garden and that eased her grief. Back in Lochland, the old king drew his last breath and died. Many of the people he had banished were pardoned and invited back to Lochland. The Cailleach received word of this, and though she had come to love her home on Eire, she still longed for Lochland and decided to return. She was sad to leave her overflowing garden, so she dug up some of it with a trowel and filled her apron pockets with the earth. On her way back to Lochland, the waves of the ocean were so strong she struggled to make her way through. In the commotion of the wild wind and waves, some of the soil, seeds, and rocks in her pockets spilled out along the way, and it's said that those clods of earth became the Outer Hebrides.

For months and years, through weather, *fuar agus garabh, grianach agus breagha* (cold and wild, sunny and lovely) I was held deep in the belly of the stories, songs, land, and the orality of these islands. Walking and listening with the singing lochs, visiting and connecting with local tradition bearers, drinking in their language—this was the warp and weft of my day. Soon enough, my head and heart were thick with Gaelic, and understanding sprouted in me as did my ability to converse (a little). As I immersed myself into learning Gaelic, and hearing it spoken around me, I was aware of the landscape opening to me in a way that was indescribable. Hearing Seumas speaking the word *eala,* meaning swan, which thrived on the islands; Donnie speaking of the *mothan,* a small, white, five-petaled flower with folkloric wisdom connected to life-affirming blessings; and *sithean,* meaning fairy knoll (and there were/are thousands listed on the Ordinance Survey maps) opened my imagination in unique and new ways. My mind was on fire as I learned Gaelic through speaking and conversation—not through a book. At that time, with my mouth and ears full of this rich language, it felt like the music of Gaelic was the same music of the landscape. In me, there was a knowing that Scottish Gaelic was a language, deeply interconnected with the more-than-human-world.

What an honor spanning seasons, weaving over years, to be gifted by glimpses of the islander's kinship with this land. To be blessed by their ways of hearing, seeing, knowing, and being in an animate world. To be claimed by tir a'mhurain, the land of bent grass, where storied layers between ancient time and present-day inform a 20th century people's knowing. Where their intimate knowing of place, and participation in living ecosystems of machair and moor, of sea and shore, of ben and hillock, of beast and bird, lichen and stone, was and still is, woven intimately with their language and lives.

Sounds of the Day

To be native to a place, we must learn its language.

– Robin Wall Kimmerer from Braiding Sweetgrass

*A*ncient and old bones of the land came to mind the first time I heard Scottish Gaelic. I was on that nascent seven-hour ferry crossing through the silver dark Minch in May 1995, bound for Lochboisdale, South Uist. In the lounge, a clutch of men were sitting in a booth, their crofters' faces, like the skerries we passed by, were scoured by sea and wind. Lying at one man's feet, a border collie slept. Their words spiked through the plumes of cigarette smoke engulfing them. The only word I understood was *ashtray*, as a man slid one across the table. The sound of their language in my ears was round and rough, brisk and lyrical—it was a language with muscle. Scottish Gaelic is a Celtic branch of the Indo-European language family and considered a Goidelic language, as are Irish and Manx, with origins in Old Irish. Most of modern-day Scotland was once Gaelic-speaking.[xxiii]

Over the years, Gaelic drew me into the landscape and landmarks of these islands. The duns (dùn), brochs (dùin), and stone circles (cearcallan cloiche), the chambered cairns (seòmarach cùirn), fairy knolls (sìthean), and standing stones (tursachan) of eons old Lewisian Gneiss, while silent in one sense, speak eloquently in another. Their language speaks of deep time, deep stories, and secret histories of the land and of ancient peoples—the Picts and Celts. These stone markers woven into the landscape are beings in their own right, voicing an engaging mutual kinship with the cycles of the sun, the moon, with life, and the very earth upholding them. They speak to the value these cycles played in the lives of ancient peoples. They speak also of protection from the seizures of storms, and the waves and waves of brutal invasions by the Norse, who left their own mark on the language and this land.

While the numbers of Scottish Gaelic speakers on the Islands in the mid-1990s were in decline, the language was still being spoken in some homes, in the shops and on the buses, particularly by those over the age of fifty. At *cèilidhean* (gatherings of music, dancing and story), Gaelic was often the only language being spoken, that I heard anyway, especially when I sat with the *cailleachan* (older women) and *bodaich* (older men). When I was out visiting, whether I was on the island of Barra to the south, or Scalpay in the north, folks always shared their stories in Gaelic first.

One midsummer's day with my analog field recorder, a packet of oatcakes, and a bottle of water in my pack, I headed out the door from where I was staying in Stilligarry to pay a visit with Mary MacRury in Loch Carnon. Maybe I'd catch a lift from a passing car, maybe not. If not, it would be a six mile walk over mostly single-track roads. A lovely walk. The last stretch of the trek was along the remote east side of the island, and the road curved and rose and fell over con-toured moorland—lapwings, sheep, and the silent bobbing of yellow flag irises thrived. Sometimes, if the wind was a gentle blow, I'd hear the call of the elusive corncrake, a bird more heard than seen, that breeds in the Western Isles. Sometimes, along this swath of moor, the eerie sound of trumpeter swans' wingbeats hummed in me for hours after.

Mary always had a fresh batch of scones with strong tea to offer. Sometimes a few of her young grandchildren sat with us, sometimes it was just the two of us, sharing bits and pieces of our lives. Always, Mary had a handful of stories to tell. That summer's day, sitting by the Rayburn in her kitchen, Mary shared this story about what happened on a nearby loch long, long ago, in Gaelic, then in English.

O chionn, tha mi cinnteach, a dhà no trì linntean air ais, bha a' fuireach a-staigh anns an Iochdar, gille òg, tapaidh, làidir, agus thug e gealladh pòsaidh do nighinn a bha a' fuireach faisg air. Ach co-dhiù thachair Iain ri nighinn eile agus ghabh e air fhèin gum b' i i sin an tè a b' fhèarr leis agus leig e sìos an nighean eile. Thug e gealladh pòsaidh dhi.

Ach co-dhiù bha e oidhche air banais ann an Gàisinnis (thall dìreach mu choinneamh an àite sa bheil mi a' fuireach an-diugh), agus bha iad a' dannsa 's gan cluich fhèin fad na h-oidhche 's nuair a bha a' bhanais seachad is i air soilleireachadh gu snog, ghabh iad sìos am mòinteach. Chaidh iad sìos Stròm, an Àird, agus ghabh iad sìos mòinteach an Iochdair agus thàinig iad gu loch – loch ris an canar an-diugh Loch Mhic Eachainn. Air an loch tha dhà na trì eileanan. Tha dùn air cuideachd 's tha mi cinnteach gun deach a cur ann san chòigeamh no an t-siathamh linn deug nuair a bha daoine a' teicheadh agus a' dol am falach anns an eilean. Ach co-dhiù, air fear dhe na h-eileanan beaga a tha air, bha eala a' nead agus 's ann a thuirt an gille,

"O, nach e bhiodh math ugh eala airson bracaist."

Agus thuirt fear dhe na gillean, (bha ceathrar aca ann, triùir ghillean eile còmhla ris is nighean ma dh' fhaoidhte), "O cha rachainn idir a-mach oir faodaidh an eala sin tionndadh ort."

"O," ars esan, "làidir 's gu bheil i tha na làmhan agamsa làidir is nì ni an gnothach oirre."

'So' dh' fhalbh e a-mach. Chuir e dheth aodach is shnàmh e a-mach. Agus nuair a bha e gu bhith aig an eilean dh' èirich an eala bhàrr na nead is thòisich i air coiseachd air an uisge, agus an ceann ùine gu math goirid, thionndaidh i na boireannach. Agus 's e am boireannach a bha innte an nighean a bha e air gealladh pòsaidh a thoit dhi, agus a leigeil sìos. Ghabh i dha ann an sin gus an do chuir i fodha e agus gun do bhàth i e.

Agus a-nis feumaidh gun robh e aig an nighinn a bha sin no aig a màthair, no aig cuideigin anns an teaghlach, gun robh dòigh aca air dèanamh air falbh leis a' ghille bhochd a bha sin air sàilleabh mar a leig e sìos iad anns an t-saoghal. Ach 's e sin an-diugh an t-ainm a tha air Loch Mhic Eachainn.

Sin mar a chuala mise an naidheachd nuair a bha mi òg.

~

Two or three centuries ago, there lived in Iochdar a young, capable, strong boy, and he became engaged to be married to a girl who lived near him. But anyway, Iain met another girl and decided that he preferred her, so he jilted the first one. He became engaged to the second girl.

But anyway, one night he was at a wedding in Gaisinnis (directly opposite where I live today) and they were dancing and having fun all night and when the wedding was finished and the day having dawned, they set off down the moor. They went down Strome, Aird, and the Iochdar moor 'til they came to a loch—a loch known today as MacEachen's Loch. There are two or three islands on the loch. There is also a fort there which I am sure was built in the 15th or 16th century when people were running away and hiding on the island. But anyway, on one of the small islands there was a swan nesting and the boy said, "Wouldn't a swan's egg be nice for breakfast?"

And one of the other boys said, (there were four of them, another three boys and perhaps a girl) "Oh, I would not go out at all because that swan is liable to turn on you."

"Oh," said he, "Strong as she is, my hands are strong and I will overcome her."

So out he went. He took off his clothes and swam out. As he was approaching the island, the swan rose up from the nest and started walking on the water, and in a very short time she turned into a woman. And the woman she now was, was the woman to whom he had promised marriage and then let down. She attacked him there 'til eventually he sank and was drowned. And now it must be that the girl, or her mother, or someone in her family, possessed some way of getting rid of that poor boy as punishment for letting them down in this life. But that is why MacEachen's Loch is so named today.

That is how I heard the story when I was quite young. [xxvi]

After my visit, in the twilight, Mary's husband, Niall gave me a lift back to Stilligarry. We drove up and over, along and through Loch Carnon, and Mary's voice, the sound of her mother tongue, rang bright in my head. Through the open car window, I heard too the layers of sound and stories rising from the wild moors and the silver-dark lochs alive in me.

Wild Moorland

... May I be an isle in the sea
May I be a hill on the shore
May I be a star in the dark time
May I be a staff to the weak ...
– The Yarrow in the Carmina Gadelica

My life altered the day I stepped off the *Lord of the Isles* ferry, —my lungs filled with salt air, my ears hummed with Scottish Gaelic—and landed in Lochboisdale, on South Uist. I woke up to an ancient and authentic way of living, as well as my voice as a woman at that time in my life.

From that beginning, as I passed under the lintel and into the peat-warm homes of the elders I came to know, there was a growing desire to live a more interconnected life; to be *of the land,* in a way I had always longed for. Those island elders became teachers and mentors in interconnection, and also in the ancient craft of oral storytelling.

Answering that call to return to Scotland and the Isles, year after year, with a sense of wonder, grit, and respect was also a holy yes to an awareness of the wild moors of my womanhood, the stone circles of my matrilineal ancestors, a sense of my own indigeneity in need of rescue, and an interconnectedness with the living land,

and sea, and sky inside me. This has taken decades to integrate, to even begin to articulate, and is still very much in process.

There are two words, neither of which exist in English, that have helped me integrate and articulate these big insights, feelings, and experiences. One is the Scottish Gaelic word, *dùthchas*, (doo-chas with the 'ch' as in the end of 'lock'). Dùthchas may have various definitions, depending on who you ask. That said, here are a few threads of meaning to consider. Dùthchas is the culture that's within you and around you. It is in your blood, bones, and DNA, and the songs sung and stories told that are passed down through families. Dùthchas is all the landscapes around you—the forests, moors, shorelines, waterways, and all the places where you grew up. It is all the beliefs that are there in those places, and dùthchas is how all that interconnects. Dùthchas is the knowing and under-standing of all this. And even though I did not grow up in Scotland, I sensed this experience through the islanders I knew. I also sensed dùthchas in my own way from a lifelong relationship with Gad, and inexplicably, through my limited relationship with Scotland.

The other is the Welsh word *hiraeth* (hear-eyeth, roll the "r") which inadequately translates in English as an experience of long-ing, a yearning for a place, a culture and time you would and could never truly know. Hiraeth has been likened to a home-sickness laced with grief and sorrow over lost or departed: land-scapes, peoples, culture, and a way of being with the world, espe-cially related to Wales.

While living in the Isles, neither of these words found me, though they were at play in me. I wonder, can hiraeth and dùthchas—while nonexistent in the English language—be sensed or known by non Welsh and Scottish Gaelic speakers? Is it possible these potent words might point to part of what is missing in peoples without a language that names these experiences? There is something to grieve here, and I wonder if there is something that could be woven into the English language going forward? All respect and gratitude to these Indigenous languages for the gift of this understanding—however limited it may be.

~

It feels important to pause here and acknowledge that my being able to travel on my own, on a shoestring, even in an exceptionally grassroots fashion, was absolutely a privilege of my white, educated, middle class 1990s circumstances. It was (and still is) a privilege for me to choose to answer the call that beckoned me to inquire and explore beyond my country of origin, and try to satisfy that inner longing for a place, other ways of life and wilderness within and without.

My familial background is steeped in very humble Midwestern roots. I was the first in my extended family, maternal and paternal, to graduate from college. Also, I was the first to leave my country of origin for reasons other than war or military service. I chose to travel abroad, and considered myself a traveler, rather than a tourist.

I am also a young woman of a long lineage of women whose expected 'work' in the world was to have babies (grandmother Magdalena, gave birth 15 times), to feed, mend, and tend to their families, to work the soil—a more than full time 'job.' Yet, the rub here is that often, for so many of my women blood ancestors, this was the only option available. After my mom graduated from high school in the late 1950s in rural North-central Wisconsin, the only options she felt she had were: marry a local man and raise a family; become a teacher, marry and raise a family; or become a nurse, marry, and raise a family. She chose the latter and over the years hinted that she would have done things differently if she felt she could have. Eventually, my mom, strong as the granite bedrock she grew up on, would step into the stream of having choice. She would choose to be part of the women's movement in the mid 1970s and divorce her husband, my dad, and become a single mother with a career as a hospital administrator.

My mom, in her life, in that era, was a cycle breaker and a model for me in choosing my path. Traveling and connecting with places and people *other* than 'my own' was part of my singular lived experience of having choice, part of my soul's education and life's path. I am forever grateful to my mom; Lorna Lou Albrecht Chipman for the gifts her cycle-breaking choices offered me.

In my own life, timing, privilege, intention, naivete, and good fortune conspired, bestowing me with the gift to answer that inner wild moor calling with a *Holy Yes*! And in having the courage and relative means to follow that *Holy Yes!* I began moving deeper into knowing my wildish self, my interconnectedness with the more-than-human world and, in hindsight, with Mystery/Spirit/Divine. And here, in my experience, lies a robust and essential freedom— a freedom that through self-knowledge, through more intimate, aware experiences with the natural world, and with the numinous, allowed me greater resilience and a more unifying experience with all that is. It is my deepest desire that this energy ripples out—affecting, touching, and inspiring others in ways singular to them. We all have our own wild moorland to experience.

Waxing Gibbous Moon in Pisces

T his week, I met the wind, and it scared the socks off me. I was in Daliburgh visiting with Cathie Walker. She is such a dear woman. How we laughed and laughed. She tells the best stories. We had tea and strùan, which is a delicious scone that is traditionally made on Michaelmas, or *Là Fhèill Mhìcheil*, in Gaelic. Michaelmas is the Feast of the Archangel Michael, celebrated near the end of September. In the Western Isles, this is traditionally celebrated by baking a special kind of cake called a *Strùan Mhìcheil*– the evening before.

The bus heading north back to Stilligarry was a wee bit early and I missed it. It was starting to get dark, and a gale was blowing in. I knew chances were good that I would catch a lift, so I continued walking out of town putting out my hand at passing cars. Most indicated with a pointing hand as they drove past, they were turning off soon and wouldn't be going straight on. In all my time on the islands, I have always, eventually, gotten a lift. Sometimes it takes a while, hours even, and it's not because folk aren't happy to help out, it's simply that there are often very few travelers on the road in these remote reaches of the Western Isles. Since I was walking on the main road out of Daliburgh, I was confident I'd get a lift soon. I walked past the Borodale Hotel and carried on out of town.

I passed by the wee loch where often a family of swans bobbed for food.

The wind was a god. The average wind speed for this time of year is around 13 knots or 15 mph, and that day on the road, it was well over 40 mph if not higher.

It was getting darker, and I carried on down the road. There was a lull in the wind, and then ten seconds later a blast came from the west! This gust smacked into me and lifted me off the tarmac, nearly bringing me down into the ditch. My heart was pounding! The immediate adrenaline rush was like a second slap. Fuck, I was so glad there wasn't a car coming. In the dark, along the road with this wild dangerous wind battering into my body, I truly felt afraid and not safe. I felt panic rising and I needed to get out of this wind. I was just about to turn around and head to Cathie's place when a car heading north pulled up and gave me lift back to Stilligarry, to home, and the warmth of hot tea with Sarah and my cozy wee room.

The next morning, the gale was still blowing, and I found myself feeling afraid to go out. What to do? After a bit, and another cuppa, I put on all the layers of clothes I had and went outside and down the road to the machair. I knew the only way to work with this fear in me was to befriend the wind and that's what I did. I gave myself to the wind. Leaning into this gale force presence, being lifted and pushed around the grassy expanse of machair, I forged a relationship with the wind.

One day, when I'm older, grayer, I shall tell this story of meeting the wild Uist wind. I've been on the path of storyteller for about three years, and mostly tell traditional tales. One day perhaps I will feel confident to tell stories from my own strange and rich life. One day ...

It's Samhain and I shall go out to the beach, in the gloaming and dance the Dashing Sargent with the wind!

I feel strong and wild!

Strùan Mhìcheil-Scones

also called Michaelmas Cake

– Adapted recipe courtesy of the late Dolly Bhop
via her daughter Anna Mhairi NicIain

Ingredients-Scone

24 Ounces self-rising flour

1 1/2 Teaspoon salt

3 Teaspoon baking powder

6 Ounces butter

1/2 Pint full cream milk (might need more if too dry)

Good sprinkling of caraway seed

Ingredients-Topping

4 Large eggs

5 Tablespoons sugar

1/2 Tin treacle (1/3 Cup)

  Can substitute equal amounts of light and dark corn syrup

Small Cup full cream milk

1/2 Teaspoon baking powder

1 Pound sieved flour (self-rising)

2 Tablespoon cooking oil

Method

Preheat oven to 350 F. Make scone by creaming butter with rest of ingredients. Remove dough from bowl and shape into one large circular form (using all of the dough) and set on an oiled baking pan. Place in the oven at 350 F for @ 22 minutes—this all comes down to eye and what the scone feels like! It should be slightly golden brown.

Make the topping while the scone is in the oven.

Break eggs into bowl, add sugar, mix using mixer till frothy, add treacle small cup of milk, and mix again for a few minutes. Add baking powder and flour (might need a wee bit more flour if too runny). Now add cooking oil.

Turn scone over, once baked and out of the oven, and cover the top side with about half the topping mixture. Bake for about 15 minutes, remove from oven, flip over (easier said than done!). Apply the rest of topping to this side of the scone. Bake for another 20 minutes. Reduce temp again in last 5 minutes on second side of topping. If getting too brown, lower the temperature.

Betwixt and Between

With the white-blush sands receiving my sole's impression,

with the roar of black waves and shining shingle,

with redshank's spangled call,

with my tongue's taste of salt-rimed lips,

with every milk-blue cockle dug,

with the cinnamon-scented bog asphodel tucked behind my left ear,

with the whistling wings of mute swans' flight,

through mackerel skies I was remembered.

Remembered into the red granite ecology of my youth,

into eagle's wide winged gaze and the long

shining waters of my life yet to come.

We are all indigenous to somewhere.

There is no landscape feature more powerful to me than the fluxing edge between land and sea, the *tràigh*, in Scottish Gaelic. There, on the numinous edge of neither and both, the known tangible earth and the fluid mystery of deep-water, a betwixt and betweenness, a liminality exists.

At this threshold place, I know an unwavering of centered calm and sublime power. This is the place where I see my true soul self most clearly revealed and reflected. This is a place that dreams the truest me.

Once I was properly initiated by this land/sea edge, deeper insights spilled out to me from the old mythlines and stories. From South Uist's folklore to the great epic Celtic myths, life's highest truths blazed: Isolde's honor, the Spey-wife's warning, the Selkie's longing, the Faerie Queen's gift, True Thomas's journey, and the Cailleach's apron emptying, drew me further through the lintel of Celticity.

In me, these old tales spun, the feral island landscapes dreamed, and the deep trove of magic firing from the Scottish Gaelic language affected my relationship with life. This multidimensional experience supported me on how I might live my precious life going forward: the choices I'd make, where I'd find/create beauty, and the direction I would steer my soul work as a storyteller/writer/teacher/mentor. This experience changed my perspectives and priorities, altering how I would listen to all living beings, and the familial roles those entities would play in my life. The way I live now: the mutual collaboration, and trust in the precious layers of life is directly derived from immersing myself into the language, the land, and the stories of these Outer Hebridean islands.

To me, Celtic indigeneity is a calling to belong to something greater, something luminous, stitched throughout the horizontal and vertical realms of life, to a living Earth. It is a coupling with the land elementals, with my soul self, and with the web that meshes, coils, and weaves us all together. My way of being in the world now has been birthed, cultured, and tempered by Celticity.

Through listening to the calling of the dynamic open moor and my engagement with the graveled Gaelic flowing from wise and foolish tongues, a responsibility travels with me now—in and beyond the Celtic lands—to actively practice a full-bodied knowing that I am in kinship with All.

Borealis Mundi

Get down and taste the earth.
The peaty-black gold of her
the grainy bones of him.
Bring them into your body,
let the ancient scent of ki enter
into the ancient passages
of your nostrils.

Your heart remembers this
smell, this taste.
One day your bones
will come to this,
Will be part of the humming
decay of this.

We are holy elixir, stardust,
an inland sea, copper flakes
from deep-time stone,
Begat before language.

New Moon in Sagittarius

Two weeks ago, while on the mainland, I was at the most excellent ceilidh with Rona Lightfoot near Inverness! So much laughter, song, story, and community! From there I was meant to travel over to the Isle of Canna for a visit with Margaret Fay Shaw, the American folklorist whose work gathering songs and stories in South Uist between 1929 and 1935 has been such an inspiration to me these past years. Unfortunately, the winter gales grounded the ferry over to Canna for many days and the window of our meeting closed. Such a shame.

I have 15 more days here in Loch Eport with Kathleen and Michael. We'll celebrate Christmas and Hogmanay, which will be such good fun! Seumas and Donnie might join us. I'm sure I'll have one more ceilidh with Cathie Walker. Oh God, then, big sigh, *bhi mi a falabh*, I'll be going away. First Edinburgh, then back to the States and a new home in Vermont! Honestly, right now my guts are in knots about this and my heart breaks even thinking about it. There have been, are presently, and will be tears flowing, and flowing, and flowing. And I know, just like the mighty gale winds, these big feelings, this great loss shall pass, right? I'll be back, one day, though it will never be like this.

Feeling festive and also sad this journey is coming to an end. Endings are hard!

~

Reflecting back on this entry—December 2018: The departure on the ferry from Lochmaddy that fresh morning in 1998 would be an ending of those long-term stays in the Outer Hebrides. I would return many more times, though only for days, and weeks, rather than months. That departure, then, was so very tender and poignant at the time, and even more so in hindsight.

The next time I returned to the isles in 2004, Donald MacDonald and Seumas MacLeod would be gone, then Donnie MacRury, then Mary MacLean, and Mary MacRury, Michael Branagan, and then Cathie Walker. So many of those who had honored me with stories and presence, would be gone. Raising a glass for absent friends!

Wool Gathering

Spiraling wider over the landscape, leaning in, treading lightly. Listening with the moors, sea, the people, their history, their aching cosmology of grief—I met a majestic ecology I am part of, and realized a forgotten reciprocation that had always been with me.

I met a labyrinth of grief. A grief that was mine and not mine.

As I walked the landscapes of Scotland, I walked with my own wild-life, aperture wider, lens clearer - my experience, a purer awareness, a singular, iterative and Indigenous expression of truth—becoming the compass, living the story and the feast I was starved for.

Remembering

Landscape is my religion.

– Norman MacCaig, The Poems of Norman MacCaig

T he leaves are holding on longer this year. Their thin petioles secure, still nursing from the mother rowan branch, still feeding. They are flaming, yoni shaped, frisking in the stiff wind, tethered in the moon's new-bright grin and the sun's departure. We know this story; how at just the right moment, the forces will conspire, when the leaf's sucking slacks and wind's tug wins. The inevitable wild release, their departure, their arrival to unfamiliar stillness, grounded to earth.

Stepping under the lintel to my old home again. Arriving back into a new departure. The Lewisian Gneiss welcomes. The bog asphodel, gorse, and bracken, the roe deer, and the salmon know. In the bough of mountain ash a spider spins for meat. The gloaming seeps, tea-staining the layering light. Those in the unseen, re-member. Gathering closer, ancestors watch.

For three weeks now, my feet have fallen upon a land that woke me up once upon a time ago. This is my first time being back here in South Uist since 2004. The thirstiest parts of me soak the poly-dimensionality of these western islands. Over tarmac and moorland, machair, and shingle, I roam in the very best company.

It is boring and cliché, and a paradox calling Scotland a homeland. And yet she is. In the immense presence of this place a marrow-deep knowing pours in; the feast of silence found within the song of the sea, the psalm of the wind in the bracken, the lapwing's skirl, and the vastness in between this cacophony. The one who burns in me to belong, cools, lands, settles a bit. A great *Ahhhhh* slips from my lips where for a moment, I'm truly at rest. Until, lifetimes of unquenchable longing begin again to niggle, chafe, and ache for a deeper communion. Is this part of the human condition or evidence that there are places that resonate with the soul? Will I always feel an outsider in this place? The one who dwells along the fringes between land and sea, between the homogenization of speaking English and the wild landscape of learning Gaelic, between the heave of 21st Century America and the weave of the cultural traditions of the Gaels?

Perhaps, being an outsider, here and in other places I've known, draws me deeper inside myself. In and further in, to a wild moorland, a flowering machair, to the singular and communal silence and the megaliths of grief inside my precious miraculous body. I am holding the mystery, the curiosity of this, and here, for now, I am part of the layers of this place, humming hallelujahs of gratitude, claimed by the familiar at-a-loss-for-words majesty.

Slanting autumn light brings out the gold in the dry-salted husks of marram grass, ceaselessly wind-stirred. Holy ochre lichen, blooded rust of spent bracken, and the mercurial hymns of shining South Uist lochs dissolve the landscape, becoming more than the sum of their parts. There is a pause. Wounds wither. A catalyst. Here is my love making with grief and longing. Here, a reckoning of the deepest love; of place, with the well of ancestral intelligence, and the felt, in the body connection with the infinite, animate more-than-human voices. Unspeakably clear. Utterly inexplicable.

Letting this recognition rise: that each separate place, hillock, vale, estuary, isthmus, knoll, moraine, and stretch of shoreline is alive and equal, just a different quilt patch of the same sprawling, mycelial weave beneath our feet and in the deep ecology of our bodies.

If nothing else, I am remembering this: the generous smile on the red-haired lass in Dr. Martins, walking up Sauchiehall Street, is the very same smile on the cashier at the gas station on Bayfield Street. The smooth pebble, green and translucent in my left palm, picked out of the north Atlantic on the cusp of an Iona beach, is the same old soul of red granite plucked off the dead-end gravel of my Wisconsin youth, now tucked into my right hand. The me of me is part of this weaving sentience.

And every woman my mother, sister, sea, my sun.
Every man my father, brother, mountain, my moon.
Every marble-white bone and stone of the
   more-than-human-world—us.
One skull, one breath, one land.

Closure

Her name is Mystery. She never looks back.
She lives in the lintel where spider spins,
He waits like raven in the cave's Basalt black wall,
Sings ragas down from the space between the stars.

Beneath the vast inky loch she stirs
in the place where most cannot breathe
joining the head and tail of Serpent, of Life.
They are a Weaver: A rash. A remedy. A disco. A chancer.
An ending. A Beginning.
The flowering of every-blessed-fuckingthing,
known and beyond knowing. A luminous liminality
between + including Death and Birth.

If we ask, with our hearts full of thorns and rose petaled stories
they will find us, lead us through the labyrinth of false belongings,
of shoulds and shouldn'ts; weave in and under and over and out
of all failed resurrections, heart attacks of longing, and a tapestry
of wonderment to a deep sleep-well-at-night peace, To a truth.
A question with 10,000 singular truth brimming "answers."
Whom do you serve?

We will close swan-white wings around flailing arms
whisper in your left ear until your eyes sting with grace,
until your knees sink to Earth, every wound bleeding,
toasting and cursing God. Follow. Follow. Follow us anyway.

Gratitudes

What does one say, here in this linear way, that does justice to the gratitudes gushing in me for so many—humans and more-than-humans? Here is my humble list, knowing there will be many who are tucked under the weave of my memory.

First, the Earth, who has held me, who is in me, who I am of. Holy miracle planet—my kin, my home, my heart. My parents, Lorna and Wayne who, for better or worse, supported my explorations of living an off-the-map life. My uncle Gary for 50 some years of unconditional love, always, even when we talk politics. To Pat for believing in me. My dear Patrick for being my anchor and co-partner in this bodacious life. To the places of this planet who I've known and who have known me: the lakes, lochs, moors, prairies, the forests, shorelines and islands, and the realms of moss, hyphae, rock, winged, scaled, rooted, and leafed ones dwelling in these places. And to the liminal places in between.

In the writing of this book, deepest thanks to Judith, April and Brianna—my fearless and inspiring writers' group. To CBAC for the grant support to share an oral storytelling of these northern tales that sweet summer of 2021.

To Franciszka Voeltz, Carter MacKenzie, Lisa Carter and Kim Blue for the sublime editing supports. To Tom Hirons, and to Ros at

Little Big Bay publishing for the 10,000 things that made this book arrive into the world, for real.

To *The Midwives:* Ann, April, Cielle, Denise G, Denise S, Erin, Gina, Jackie P, Jackie S, Judith, Kay, Kelly, Millie, Nina, Patty, Samantha, Kathar, Rachel and Theresa—the women who span decades and decades of my life—who witnessed, listened, and cheered me through the labor pains of birthing this book.

To my dear friends from the Isles of Barra, South Uist, Benbecula, Grimsay, North Uist, Berneray, Scalpay, and Harris for allowing me to be in the presence of your lives, your language, your stories, and the way the wild Hebridean landscapes dreams you.

To the last-ditch efforts of the crowd-funding cohort: Tom, Carter, Vic, Tony, Jane, and Susan. Thank you, thank you three bags full. And to you dear Reader, deep bow for arriving here, choosing this!

About the Author

Tracy Chipman (she/her/they) has traveled to the island of St Kilda, (without boat or airplane), moved 22 times in the span of 25 years, and holds a Master's Degree in Vedic Science. She has worked as an early childhood educator, a marketing director for a professional musical theater company, and a marmalade cook in Ireland's Burren. She, along with her partner Patrick and black cat,

Pippin, live in gratitude on Anishinaabe lands, stewarding a small holding of holy boreal forest, near the long-shining waters of Lake Superior.

The breadth and depth of stories, liminal places, and the complex constellations of human experience have always been magnetizing draws for Tracy. In 1995 she stepped onto the path of storyteller under a hazel tree and has continued to engage in reciprocity with the wild landscapes of stories, place and the awe and rupture of being human through her work as an oral storyteller, writer, somatics instructor, story guide and mentor.

Borealis Mundi is her first book. Learn more about her work, join her mailing list and read her latest blogs at www.tracychipman.net.

Endnotes

i David Abram, writer, ecologist, activist, philosopher coined the phrase "the more-than-human world" in his book *The Spell of the Sensuous.*

ii Lyric line from Kae Tempest, *Holy Elixir.* https://www.kaetempest.co.uk/

iii Zora Neale Hurston, *Their Eyes Were Watching God,* used with permission

iv Lake Superior—the world's largest freshwater lake by surface area—is 31,700 square miles (82,100 square kilometres), or roughly the size of Maine and holds 10 percent of the world's surface fresh water. Lake Superior's 3 quadrillion gallons are enough to cover both North and South America under a foot of water. Here's another (preposterous) way to think about it: downing half a gallon of water daily, it would take you 16.4 trillion years to drink Lake Superior. Or the entire world population of 7 billion people, each person drinking half a gallon per day, could together polish off Lake Superior in 2,348 years. https://www.lakesuperior.com

v Ki, from Robin Wall Kimmerer's book *Braiding Sweetgrass* as a relational pronoun for the more-than-human world, the natural world.

vi https://www.anishinaabemdaa.com/#/

vii Duck for the Oyster—a Wisconsin based contra band that brought joy to many, many over the years!

viii Roslyn Nelson, *Love Stories of the Bay* on Amazon.com

ix Milwaukee artist Mary Nohl lived along Lake Michigan in what many call "the witch's house." This iconic sculpture gallery has been a historic and powerful landmark in the greater Milwaukee area for decades.

x Samhain is one of the sacred festival days connected with pre-Christian culture. Other Wheel of the Year days include Winter Solstice, Imbolc, Vernal Equinox, Beltane, Summer Solstice and Lughnasa.

xi Ojibwemowin is the language of the Ojibwe or Anishinaabeg peoples. Anishinaabemowin is the Indigenous name used by the Anishinaabe peoples to refer to their languages. It literally means "original people's language." Since Anishinaabe is a general term used by several Algonquian speaking tribes of the Great Lakes and prairie regions, "Anishinaabemowin" (or one of its many spelling variants like Anishinabemowin, Anishnabemowin, Nishnaabemowin, etc.) can sometimes be used to refer to more than one distinct language, such as the Ojibwe, Algonquin, Ottawa, Oji-Cree, or Potawatomi languages. These languages are all related but are not identical; the situation is similar to languages like Spanish, French, Portuguese, and Italian in Europe, all of which share many features yet still are not interchangeable. http://www.native-languages.org/definitions/anishinaabemowin.html

xii John O'Donohue, Irish poet/philosopher https://www.johnodonohue.com/

xiii Sophie Strand from *The Flowering Wand: Rewilding the Sacred Masculine,* used with permission. add period after permission. https://sophiestrand.com/

xiv Martin Shaw, from *Small Gods,* Used with permission, https://drmartinshaw.com

xv https://www.wpr.org/how-did-wisconsin-get-its-name-well-its-complicated

xvi Communion of Subjects from a quote by eco-theologian Thomas Barry "The universe is primarily a communion of subjects not a collection of objects." Thomas Barry, *Earth Community, Resurgence,* No.244, September/October 2007

xvii In early May 2016, a wildfire began in northwestern Alberta,

Canada, southwest of Fort McMurray. The fire spread across northern Alberta and into Saskatchewan, burned out of control until early July then smoldered until early August. The wildfire spread across approximately 1,500,000 acres, destroying habitat and wildlife in its path. The fire was suspected to have been caused by humans in a remote area about nine miles from Fort McMurray, but no official cause has been determined to date. It was the costliest disaster in Canadian history. https://en.wikipedia.org/wiki/2016_Fort_McMurray_wildfire

xviii Shared with permission. www.chelanharkin.com

xix A retelling of David's story, shared with permission. www.davidcampbellstoryteller.com

xx Machair is a Gaelic word meaning fertile low lying grassy plain. This is the name given to one of the rarest habitats in Europe which only occurs on exposed western coasts of Scotland and Ireland. There are Machair habitats on the western shores throughout the islands. https://www.visitouterhebrides.co.uk

xxi Sin a gade, a Scottish Gaelic word, often translates as, "That's it" as in "That's the end, there is no more." Sin a gade is often heard in use at the end of a good story.

xxii From *Carmina Gadelica*: a compendium of prayers, hymns, charms, incantations, blessings, literary folkloric poems and songs, proverbs, lexical items, historical anecdotes, natural history observations, and miscellaneous lore gathered in the Gaelic-speaking regions of Scotland between 1860 and 1909.

xxiii Tom Hirons, from *Falconer's Joy*. Used with permission: https://tomhirons.com

xxiv tracychipman.net/hebridean-folklore-project whose mission was to help keep Scottish Gaelic folklore alive and accessible. It was common practice in the 1990s and earlier for many universities to keep field recordings inaccessible to even those who gave the folklore recordings. Since then, this has shifted somewhat and some institutions are more conscious of the value of making these archives accessible.

xxv *Cailleach Sgàire* was recorded by Norman MacLeod of Leverburgh Harris. Permission given to share. https://dasg.ac.uk/audio/view/s/mot/ norman%20macleod/ Stories_from_Leverburgh

xxvi Permission to share story given by Mary Johnson MacRury and transcription into Gaelic and translation into English by Murdo Nickelson.

Ponderings

Reflect, ponder or meditate on your how experiences of place, loss, and grace have shaped your life.

1/ Where are the geographical places that pull you back again and again? What is it about these places that move you, keep you coming back?

2/ Who are your Land,* Blood, and Soul Ancestors and what is your relationship with each? How might you explore this more deeply?

3/ Some years ago, a very wise woman who grew up in Beirut, after hearing the story of my losses, asked—*Is your grief clean?* This was a lightning bolt for me. Is your grief clean?

4/ What landscapes offer you solace in the rupture and awe of life?

5/ What does it mean to you to be interconnected—a small part of the whole that is the living animate world? Is this a concept or your direct experience? (No wrong answers here.)

6/ If you were to make the dark experiences of your life into art, what might that look like? I am celebrating your first and/or continued steps into this!

*If you are curious to know the Indigenous people who inhabited your home places this is a helpful website: https://native-land.ca/

Made in the USA
Monee, IL
15 April 2023

31887513R00115